NARROW GAUGE MEMORIES

The Locomotives

by Steve McNicol

© 1993

Published by
Railmac Publications

P.O. Box 290, Elizabeth,
South Australia 5112
Telephone: (08) 255 9446
Facsimile: (08) 287 0696

Printed by
Kitchener Press Pty Ltd
7-11 Provident Avenue, Glynde
South Australia 5070

RMPN 96

National Library of Australia Card Number and ISBN
ISBN 0-949817-87-2

CONTENTS

K52 shunts T254 onto the turntable at Peterborough, 1929.

(Government of South Australia)

400 class No. 406 in full cry on Belalie bank in the late 1960s.   *(Roger Currie)*

INTRODUCTION

In the first two volumes of this planned trilogy we indulged ourselves in the nostalgia and romance that was the old Peterborough Division narrow gauge. We spoke to the personalities that worked the locomotives and the photographers who relayed a few brief words on their exploits and impressions. But now, in this third volume, we have a more clinical in depth study of the locomotive types that could be found on the narrow gauge. Class histories and technical details will ensure this book becomes a valuable reference source for future historians.

To conclude this series we are producing one extra volume *Narrow Gauge Memories - the Experience*. However, we are dropping the '20 Years On' from the title as it will go outside the bounds of the original series concept.

We have also been asked about producing some books on the Port Lincoln and Mount Gambier Divisions and it is our intention to cover both these divisions and the former Western Division, in a new series of books entitled *South Australian Railways Narrow Gauge Journal*. The first title is due for release during 1993.

Returning to the book in hand it has been a long time since I have been involved in a project with such enthusiasm and this is mainly due to the help from all of those who have contributed to these 'narrow gauge memories'. I feel we have accomplished what we set out to do and more. We have, over twenty years later, recorded for posterity those machines we knew and loved and that were an integral part of the charm of the old narrow gauge. We have proven the narrow gauge will never be forgotten - it will live on forever in the hearts of all those who were lucky enough to have savoured its many moods.

Steve McNicol
Adelaide
January 1992

* * * * * * * * * * *

Front cover: T198 spent its last years shunting at Peterborough as its mechanical condition excluded it from mainline work. Its sediment stained boiler adding some unusual colouring to the normally dull black paint, 24th November 1969. (Steve McNicol)

NOTES ON THE USE OF THIS BOOK

The general layout of this book covers one locomotive class at a time. Details provided for each class are; a condensed history, technical information, and finally a list of locomotive numbers, builder and builder's number, date entered service and date condemned. Some notable features of particular locomotives within the class can be found in the main text.

The dates condemned are official 'paper' dates and in some cases bear little relation to when a locomotive was taken out of traffic. For instance some T class were stored unserviceable for a number of years before being condemned. Others were condemned, but lingered in depots for some years before being cut up for scrap. In some cases the condemned date may refer to when a locomotive was officially withdrawn or sold.

Where locomotives are referred to as stored they could have been simply parked, out of use, or stored on a siding never to run again.

"In service" refers to the date the locomotive entered service on the South Australian Railways. There may be slight variations in the dates recorded in this book due to differing records. As an example, one source lists T180 as entering traffic on 13/12/1903; another gives 21/2/1903. However, it actually started work on 16/2/1903. "In service" can be a paper date, ie. despatched from Islington workshops, or the date of arrival in Peterborough, or the official date of entry into service after initial trials. To further complicate the issue, when secondhand locomotives were purchased they did not always enter traffic immediately; some needing an overhaul, in which case the in service date may actually be a purchased date. With the passage of time and loss of records it is hard to confirm what the actual dates refer to. They should therefore be taken as approximate dates only.

Dimensions and capacities. The dimensions given usually refer to the locomotive type in its final form. Cylinder dimensions for steam locomotives are set out thus; number of cylinders, inside (I) or outside (O) of frame, followed by the cylinder diameter and stroke.

Lengths given for locomotives are all over couplings. In some instances the overall length, ie. over front cow catcher, could be 1 foot 5½ inches longer.

Total refers to the total number of locomotives built of that particular class. However, they may not all have been in service at the same time.

As all locomotives were built before the introduction of the metric system imperial measurements have been used throughout this book. However, we have provided the following conversion chart for those wishing to know the metric equivalents.

Imperial	to (X)	Metric	to (X)	Imperial
miles	1.6093	kilometres	.6214	miles
feet	.30479	metres	3.28084	feet
inches	25.3995	millimetres	.03937	inches
gallons	4.5435	litres	.21997	gallons
tons	1.01605	tonnes	.984207	tons
horsepower	.7457	kilowatts	1.34102	horsepower
pounds	.45359	kilograms	2.20462	pounds

This book covers the narrow gauge locomotives owned and operated by the South Australian Railways. It does not include ex Commonwealth Railways types, or Australian National locomotives transferred to work the Peterborough to Quorn and Gladstone to Wilmington lines after the amalgamation of the ex S.A.R. country lines and Australian National in March 1978. A.N. locomotives transferred to the Port Lincoln Division are also excluded.

Railcars have not been included in this publication. However, they can be found in the Railmac publication *S.A.R. Railcars (1920 - 1975)*.

S.A.R. No. 0 at Terowie, circa 1892. *(Author's collection)*

100 years later No. 0 (as B.H.P. No. 2) was photographed preserved at Mt. Laura Homestead, Whyalla, 20th August 1992. *(Steve McNicol)*

South Australian Railways No. 0 has a very interesting history. It is one of three similar locomotives which ended their days working for the Broken Hill Proprietary Co. Ltd., at Whyalla. There were in fact thirteen known locomotives of this type built by Beyer Peacock & Co., of Manchester, England. Two were supplied to the Minas & Rio Railway in 1881, eight were ordered by the Alcoy & Gandia Railway in South East Spain (which were delivered during 1890-91) and of course the three Australian locomotives.

The design is basically a tank version of the popular Y class tender locomotives. The rear of the frame was extended, a coal bunker added and an extra Bissell truck was placed below it to complete the changes. In this form it was quite well proportioned and a very useful locomotive for shunting and short haul work.

The story of No. 0 began when B.H.P. ordered a locomotive for use at their mine and smelter in Broken Hill. Given the builders No. 3357 by Beyer Peacock (their works order No. 7439) it arrived at Port Adelaide on 8th August 1891. It was assembled at Islington workshops for B.H.P and then despatched by rail to Broken Hill on 28th August.

On arrival it was found to be too heavy for their existing track and arrangements were made with the S.A.R. to exchange it for V class 0-4-4WT No. 11. It was transferred to the S.A.R. in July 1892 and assumed the road No. 0.

During its short period on the S.A.R. it was based on the Peterborough Division and saw some use on the *Broken Hill Express* between Terowie and Peterborough. To enable No. 0 to undertake main line work it had to haul a water gin to supplement its water supply.

Meanwhile B.H.P. had ordered another small locomotive from Nasmyth Wilson, which arrived in Broken Hill on 12th February 1893. Vll was no longer required and arrangements were made to return it to the S.A.R., in exchange for No. 0. This occurred about March 1893.

As the Nasmyth Wilson locomotive was giving satisfactory service and No. 0 was still regarded as too heavy for the track it was hired to the Silverton Tramway Co., who at the time were short of motive power and were in fact believed to have been using horses for some shunting. It was given their road number 6. However, B.H.P. then took over the furnace operations of British Broken Hill Pty. Ltd., and Block 14 (both were wholly owned subsidiaries of B.H.P.) and required a shunting locomotive. It was recalled from the Silverton Tramway and became B.H.P. Co. No. 2 in September 1893.

On 23rd July 1902 it was transferred to Hummock Hill (Whyalla), retaining its number 2, and commenced hauling iron ore from Iron Knob to Whyalla. It continued in this capacity until displaced by the Baldwin locomotives from 1914. It then worked as a shunting and standby locomotive at Whyalla until withdrawn in April 1962. Luckily it wasn't fed to the blast furnace, but instead was donated to the Whyalla City Corporation who placed it on display on the foreshore in August 1962. In 1983 it was moved to Mt. Laura Homestead where it was again put on display.

The other two B.H.P. locomotives were numbered 2A (b/n 5125 of 1908) and their 2nd No. 3 (b/n 3170 of 1890). 2A was scrapped in 1962, but No. 3 is now owned by the Pichi Richi Railway and is stored at Quorn.

Introduced	:	7/1892 (S.A.R.)	Heating Surface	:	
Builder	:	Beyer Peacock	Tubes	:	708.46sq ft.
Driving Wheel	:	3ft 3in.	Superheater	:	-
Bogie Wheel	:	2ft 0in.	Firebox	:	69.48sq ft.
Weight in W.O.	:	34tons	Grate Area	:	13.67sq ft.
Max. Axle Load	:	7tons 16cwt.	Boiler Pressure	:	140Ib./sq in.
Length	:	28ft 4in.	Tractive Effort	:	12,154Ib.
Water	:	600 gallons	Cylinders	:	2(O) 14½ x 20in.
Total	:	1 (S.A.R.)	Coal	:	40 cubic feet

No.	Bldr./No.	In Service	Returned	Notes
0	BP/3357	7/1892	3/1893	Preserved at Whyalla

U class 2-6-0 No.1 at Laura.   *(S.A. Archives)*

U Class   2-6-0

The first narrow gauge railway was opened between Port Wakefield and Hoyles Plains (Hoyleton) on 1st January 1870. For the first few years it was worked solely by horse power. Although the railway was an improvement over the early cart tracks, especially when crossing the bogs to the east of Balaklava, horse power was still slow and limited the effectiveness in which stores and produce could be transported.

A second isolated narrow gauge line was opened from Port Pirie (Ellen Street) inland to Crystal Brook on 10th December 1875, while the Port Wakefield to Hoyleton line was extended to Blyth on 1st March 1876. It was inevitable that with the continued growth of these lines that steam power would eventually have to be introduced.

The South Australian Railways placed an order with Beyer Peacock & Co., for eight small

2-6-0 tender locomotives to work on these lines and they were constructed during 1875 (BP works order No. 3267). They arrived aboard the vessel *North* and were placed in traffic during 1876. They were given road numbers 1 to 8, with 1 to 4 being allotted to the Port Pirie line and 5 to 8 the Port Wakefield line. Nos. 2, 5 and 7 were officially placed in service in April 1876, followed by 1, 3 and 4 in May, No. 6 in June and finally No. 8 in August that same year.

As further narrow gauge lines were constructed and traffic increased, the slightly more powerful W class were introduced, replacing the U class on most mainline work and relegating them to shunting and construction trains. Often, after being used on construction trains, the U class were found work in general traffic until sufficient new locomotives could be provided to replace them.

As each locomotive had an interesting life the following summary of known events is given below;

No. 1 was used by the contractors who were constructing the Gladstone to Laura line during 1884. It later returned to the Western Division at Port Wakefield and was condemned in December 1904.

No. 2 was shipped to Port Augusta in 1882 to work on the Great Northern Railway system, but returned the following year to Port Pirie. By 1892 it was based at Port Wakefield. No. 2 was first condemned on 15th May 1906, but was later rebuilt and reissued to traffic on 6th December 1911. It was transferred to the Port Lincoln Division on 27th February 1915 and then worked for the construction branch on the Wandana to Penong railway from 20th September 1922. This railway was completed in February 1924 and it was withdrawn on 1st November 1924 and sold.

No. 3 was condemned on 7th September 1904, but reissued to traffic at Port Wakefield in October 1906. It was transferred to the Port Lincoln Division on 26th March 1915. It was condemned in May 1929 and sold to H. Morrell for scrap on 29th August 1929.

No. 4 was transferred to Port Wakefield in 1887, rebuilt during February 1898 and then hired to the Wallaroo Mining Company from 9th July 1902 until some time in 1903. It was condemned the following year.

No. 5 was rebuilt in August 1898 and condemned in July 1926. Apparently it spent most of its life on the Western Division.

No. 6 was used by the contractor on the Balaklava to Hamley Bridge line. It was rebuilt in June 1894, transferred to Port Lincoln on 8th March 1915 and withdrawn from service in December 1925. It was condemned on 17th May 1929 and sold to H. Morrell for scrap on 29th August 1929.

No. 7 was rebuilt in June 1897. It was sold to the Tasmanian Copper Company for use on its colliery railway on 25th May 1907. Shortly afterwards the mine closed and U7 was repurchased by the S.A.R. on 28th February 1908. It was again sold on 23rd November 1909 to the contractor of the Laura and Booleroo Centre railway. Repurchased by S.A.R. in 1910 it was finally sold to Atkinson and Finlayson of Western Australia. There it survived until March 1955.

No. 8 had a rather uneventful life compared to the rest of the class and was condemned in December 1904.

Unfortunately no example of the U class survives and even photographs of them are scarce.

Introduced	:	1876	Heating Surface	:	
Builder	:	Beyer Peacock	Tubes	:	492.09 sq ft.
Driving Wheel	:	3ft 3in.	Superheater	:	-
Bogie Wheel	:	2ft 0in.	Firebox	:	45.42 sq ft.
Weight in W.O.	:	30tons 3cwt.	Grate Area	:	9.76sq ft.
Max. Axle Load	:	5tons 3cwt. (loco)	Boiler Pressure	:	130 1b./sq in.
Length	:	34ft 6½in.	Tractive Effort	:	7,532 1b.
Water	:	850 gallons	Cylinders	:	2(O) 12 x 20in.
Total	:	8	Coal	:	2tons 6cwt.

No.	Bldr./No.	In Service	Condemned	Notes
1	BP/1499	5/1876	12/12/1904	Issued to Port Pirie
2	BP/1505	4/1876	1/11/1924	Issued to Port Pirie
3	BP/1503	5/1876	17/5/1929	Issued to Port Pirie
4	BP/1506	5/1876	12/12/1904	Issued to Port Pirie
5	BP/1500	4/1876	7/1926	Issued to Port Wakefield
6	BP/1504	6/1876	17/5/1929	Issued to Port Wakefield
7	BP/1501	4/1876	1906	Issued to Port Wakefield
8	BP/1502	8/1876	12/12/1904	Issued to Port Wakefield

Builders photograph of V class No. 146. (Author's collection)

V Class

0-4-4WT

Shortly after the opening of the first narrow gauge lines in the north another isolated line was completed in the South East, from Kingston to Naracoorte. This railway was over 52 miles long and also used horses until the first steam locomotives arrived in 1877.

The S.A.R. ordered four locomotives from Beyer Peacock & Co. (BP works order No. 3408) in 1876 specifically for the Kingston line. They were shipped aboard the vessel *South Australian* and were issued to traffic during 1877, assuming the road numbers 9 to 12. Looking more like toys these diminutive locomotives were not very successful on this line, even with its limited traffic. It was also necessary to attach a water gin when they worked on the main line. In fact, as soon as the W class arrived 10, 11 and 12 were put into storage at Kingston depot, while No. 9 was relegated to shunting only.

These three locomotives were then transferred and used for light shunting duties on jetties and wharves. With their light axle load and short wheelbase they were ideally suited for this type of work. In fact, when additional shunting locomotives were required in connection with the increasing Barrier ore traffic four more V class were built by the Gawler firm of James Martin & Co. They were placed in traffic on the Northern Division during 1893.

They were unique little locomotives and each one had an interesting career. Individual locomotive details are provided below;

No. 9, unlike the other three locomotives, remained at Kingston and was used for shunting until 1888. It was then transferred to the Northern Division. It was rebuilt in 1896. On 8th February 1912 it was sold to the S.A. Department of Mines, but was repurchased and put back into service on 21st January 1914. It then spent the rest of its working life at Peterborough and at least in its latter years was one of the shed pilots in Peterborough roundhouse, affectionately known as the "roundhouse rat". It was taken out of traffic around 1953 and then stored at Islington until May 1955. It was then moved to Naracoorte where it was preserved in Pioneer Park. A few years ago it was renovated and a wooden shed and platform were built around it to display the locomotive and at the same time help protect it from the elements.

No. 10. In 1882 No. 10 was transferred to Wallaroo for shunting duties on the jetty. It was rebuilt in July 1894 and hired to the Wallaroo Mining Company from 1902 to 1904. It was hired to the State Electricity Commission of Victoria at Yallourn from 25th October 1921 until October 1922. It then returned to the Northern Division at Peterborough until 10th November 1937 when it was sold to the S.A. Harbours Board and put to work at Port Germein. It was used until April 1939 and put into storage until 1954. It was cut up at Port Germein.

No. 11 was transferred from the South East to Port Wakefield in 1885. It went to Port Pirie in November 1890 and was rebuilt in October 1891. On 1st July 1892 it was exchanged with a B.H.P. Co. locomotive (which became S.A.R. No. 0) until March 1893 when they were both returned to their original owners. It was used for shunting on the Western Division, but when this division was converted to broad gauge it was sold, minus boiler, to A.H. Russell of Melbourne on 11th August 1924. It spent time at Yallourn and Noojee before being cut up around 1939.

No. 12. In 1882 V12 was transferred to Port Pirie for shunting. It was rebuilt in December 1892 and then condemned on 17th September 1904. It was reissued to traffic and sent to the Port Lincoln Division on 14th June 1910. There it remained until it was condemned in 1940.

No. 143 was the first of the James Martin batch built during 1893. It was issued to the Northern Division. No. 143 was hired by the Wallaroo mines and smelter from 1906 to 1908, after which it returned to jetty shunting at Wallaroo.

V146 and V9 survived into the 1950s as shed pilots at Peterborough. (Ron Stewien)

V146, Peterborough. (Ron Stewien)

With gauge conversion it was sold to A.H. Russell of Melbourne on 11th August 1924 and used at Yallourn (Vic.) and then by the Goodwood Timber & Railway Company, Noojee (Vic.). It was scrapped in 1939.

No. 144. After initially working on the Northern Division it was sold to the S.A. Harbours Board on 25th September 1906. It was reconditioned at Glanville Dockyard and then sent to Port Germein where it worked until June 1937.

No. 145, like 143, also worked at Wallaroo for most of its life on the South Australian Railways and was sold to A.H. Russell together with Nos. 11 and 143. It was scrapped in 1939.

No. 146 was issued to the Northern Division and was painted green and cream in 1938. It spent its remaining life as shed pilot, in company with No. 9, at Peterborough until withdrawn in 1953. It was cut up at Islington in August 1954.

Introduced	:	1877	Heating Surface	:
Builder	:	BP & JM	Tubes	:	231.31sq ft.
Driving Wheel	:	3 feet	Superheater	:	-
Bogie Wheel	:	1ft 9in.	Firebox	:	25.62sq ft.
Weight in W.O.	:	15tons 13cwt.	Grate Area	:	4.66sq ft.
Max. Axle Load	:	4tons 7cwt.	Boiler Pressure	:	130lb./sq in.
Length	:	21ft 3 3/4in.	Tractive Effort	:	4,155lb.
Water	:	300 gallons	Cylinders	:	2(O) 9½ x 15in.
Total	:	8	Coal	:	12cwt.

No.	Bldr./No.	In Service	Condemned	Notes
9	BP/1597	2/1877	16/4/1955	Preserved at Naracoorte
10	BP/1598	2/1877	10/11/1937	Last worked at Port Germein
11	BP/1599	1/1877	16/7/1924	Scrapped 1939
12	BP/1619	5/1877	1/3/1940	Last worked at Port Lincoln
143	JM/67	20/9/1893	5/7/1924	Scrapped 1939
144	JM/68	27/10/1893	25/9/1906	Last worked at Port Germein
145	JM/69	1/11/1893	5/7/1924	Scrapped 1939
146	JM/70	2/12/1893	5/1953	Last worked at Peterborough

W & Wx Classes   2-6-0

Shortly after the arrival of the eight U class the S.A.R. ordered some additional, but slightly larger locomotives for the rapidly expanding narrow gauge systems. Between 1878 and 1883 thirty five of the W class were placed in traffic. They were all built by Beyer Peacock & Co., (BP works orders Nos. 3591, 3668, 3698, 6027 and 6155) and their arrival allowed some of the U class to be relegated to shunting and construction train work.

The first two W class were delivered to the Port Pirie to Jamestown line. They were followed by deliveries to the Beachport to Mount Gambier line and to Port Augusta for working on the Great Northern Railway, while Nos. 29 and 30 were issued to the Kingston to Naracoorte line to replace the V class 0-4-4 tank locomotives. Some went directly to contractors without being taken into S.A.R. stock, but they were later purchased by the S.A.R.

One of the class, No. 22, was sold to Barry, Brooks & Fraser on 16th May 1881 for work on construction trains. It was repurchased in August 1882 and given the new road number 56 as the number 22 had already been re-allocated to another new W class.

They were found on just about all narrow gauge lines and were the first locomotives on the Palmerston (Port Darwin) to Pine Creek railway in the Northern Territory, which at the time was owned and operated by the S.A.R. On the 1st January 1911 the Palmerston to Pine Creek and Port Augusta to Oodnadatta lines were transferred to the Commonwealth. While the S.A.R. still operated the line towards Oodnadatta (extended by C.R. to Alice Springs) until 1926 the motive power on the Palmerston railway was taken over by the Commonwealth. In all seven W class went to the Commonwealth Railways, most directly, but some via contractors.

S.A.R. No.	To C.R.	C.R.No.	Withdrawn C.R.	Notes
13	1/1/1911	NF2	12/1939	Preserved at Darwin
21	1/1/1911	NF3	3/1929	
35	1/1/1911	NF7 (part)	4/1944	Used for parts for NF7
36	1/1/1911	NF4	7/1928	
41	1/1/1911	NF7 (part)	as 35	Used for parts for NF7
53	1916	NF5	12/1945	Purchased from contractors
54	1916	NF6	19/2/1942	Blown into Darwin Harbour

Nos. 35 and 41 were in such a bad condition when obtained by the C.R. that they were both dismantled and one good one made from the parts. NF7 did not enter service until 1917.

No. 54 (as C.R. NF6) was blown into Darwin Harbour during a Japanese air raid on 19th February 1942 and was never retrieved.

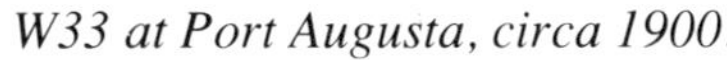

W33 at Port Augusta, circa 1900.　　　　　　　　　　　　　　*(S.A. Archives)*

Wx39 at Islington, 1904.   (Author's collection)

The W class were popular with contractors, quite often being used for a year or so on construction trains and then afterwards being sold back to the S.A.R. The following lists known movements of contractors locomotives.

No.	Sold to	Date sold	Returned	Notes
21	C & E Millar	7/1888	12/1889	Palmerston
22(1st) see No. 56				
22(2nd)	C & E Millar	30/6/1886	-	W.A.G.R A21
23	Barry Brooks & Fraser	5/1880	8/1882	Port Augusta
	C & E Millar	7/9/1886	26/9/1886	
32	C & E Millar	6/1878	7/1879	Beachport
	C & E Millar	9/9/1880	7/1882	Mt. Gambier
36	C & E Millar	1/1888	12/1889	Cockburn
38	Baxter & Saddler	3/3/1896	-	Sold to Bunnings
39	Moore, Blanch & Co.	19/6/1886	-	Naracoorte
	Construction Branch	10/1887	2/1891	
41	C & E Millar	26/9/1886	12/1889	Named *Port Darwin*
42	Construction Branch	10/1885	5/1891	
43	Construction Branch	10/1885	2/1891	
	Baxter & Saddler	7/2/1896	-	Sold to Bunnings
53	Barry Brooks & Fraser	1878	8/1882	Port Augusta
	Construction Branch	21/1/1907	11/1907	Port Lincoln
	Teesdale Smith	12/1911	-	To C.R. NF5
54	Barry Brooks & Fraser.	1878	8/1882	
	C & E Millar.	3/1887	12/1889	
	Construction Branch	1/1907	11/1907	Port Lincoln
	Teesdale Smith	26/1/1912	-	To C.R. NF6
55	Barry Brooks & Fraser	1878	8/1882	Port Augusta
56	Barry Brooks & Fraser	16/5/1881	8/1882	Sold as No.22 (1st)

The W class were very versatile and with their light axle loading could be used on some lines on which the heavier Y class were not permitted. However, as more Y class became available they were replaced on main line work.

Wx No. 17 was involved in an incident in the South East that could have caused the loss of life, but fortunately the driver and fireman were very lucky and received only a strained back and lacerations. On 2nd February 1914 No. 17 was about to depart Mount Gambier with the 2.15pm train to Wolseley when its boiler exploded. The force of the explosion was tremendous with the locomotive's dome being hurled 60 yards from the engine and one of its piston rods bent under the sudden release of pressure. This, and NF6 being blown into Darwin Harbour, were the only two serious incidents known to have involved this class of locomotive.

Seventeen of the class were rebuilt with larger boilers between 1903 and 1912 and classified Wx. The locomotives concerned were Nos. 15, 17, 18, 19, 20, 25, 26, 28, 29, 31, 33, 34, 37, 39, 40, 55 and 56. This extended their useful life by at least another twenty five years. Three of the class, Nos. 18, 37 and 56, survived on the Kingston to Naracoorte branch until gauge conversion was completed in 1959.

No. 18 worked the last narrow gauge goods from Kingston to Naracoorte on 12th March 1959. It was handed over to the town of Naracoorte on 17th April 1959 and placed on display in Pioneer Park with V9. It was transferred to the Pichi Richi Railway at Quorn in July 1985 for eventual restoration to working order.

The other two survivors in the South East were transferred to Islington, but were unfortunately scrapped in January 1961.

Commonwealth Railways NF2 (formerly S.A.R. No. 13) was stored in Darwin for a number of years. It was put on display in Darwin Primary School grounds in May 1957, but was moved to Smith Street, Darwin in 1974 and again to Fannie Bay Jail Museum in Darwin during 1983.

Two W class tenders (tender Nos. 9 and 13) were still at Peterborough in May 1959. As they were only small, one was used coupled to a Y class to allow both the Y and a T class onto the roundhouse turntable at the same time. The last Y, No. 97, used a W class tender until near the end of steam when its original larger tender was refitted while it hauled mainline enthusiasts' specials.

When Wx dimensions differ from those of the W class they are identified separately below.

Introduced	:	1878	Heating Surface	:	
	:	1903 (Wx)	Tubes	:	498.68sq ft.
Builder	:	Beyer Peacock	Superheater	:	-
Driving Wheel	:	3ft 3in.	Firebox	:	45.42sq ft.
Bogie Wheel	:	2ft 0in.		:	49.32sq ft.(Wx)
Weight in W.O.	:	29tons 18cwt.	Grate Area	:	9.76sq ft.
	:	31tons 5cwt.(Wx)	Boiler Pressure	:	130lb./sq in.
Max. Axle Load	:	5tons 3cwt. (loco)		:	145lb./sq in.(Wx)
	:	5tons 11cwt.(Wx)	Tractive Effort	:	8,159lb.
Length	:	35ft 1 3/4in.		:	9,101lb.(Wx)
Water	:	850 gallons	Cylinders	:	2(O) 12 x 20in.
Total	:	35 (17 conv. Wx)	Coal	:	2tons 6cwt.

Wx56 photographed while working in the South East.   *(Ron Stewien)*

No.	Bldr./No.	In Service	Rebuilt Wx	Condemned	Notes
13	BP/1715	2/1878	-	1/1/1911	To C.R. NF2
14	BP/1716	2/1878	-	17/5/1929	Sold for scrap 8/1929
15	BP/1719	11/1878	22/1/1904	2/1927	
16	BP/1720	11/1878	-	12/12/1904	
17	BP/1819	12/1879	7/9/1905	17/8/1927	Cut up 14/4/1928
18	BP/1820	2/1880	12/6/1911	17/3/1959	Preserved at Quorn
19	BP/1728	12/1879	14/5/1903	2/1927	
20	BP/1727	1/1880	11/6/1903	1/1956	Cut up 4/1956
21	BP/1800	1/1880	-	1/1/1911	To C.R. NF3
22 2nd	BP/2123	8/1882	-	30/6/1886	W.A.G.R. A21
23	BP/1801	12/1879	-	12/12/1904	
24	BP/1722	5/1880	-	12/12/1904	
25	BP/1723	6/1881	7/7/1903	17/5/1929	Sold for scrap 8/1929
26	BP/1724	6/1881	11/10/1905	17/5/1929	Sold for scrap 8/1929
27	BP/1802	1/1880	-	17/5/1929	Sold for scrap 8/1929
28	BP/1726	1/1880	31/3/1906	17/5/1929	Sold for scrap 8/1929
29	BP/1850	10/1879	10/12/1903	17/5/1929	Sold for scrap 8/1929
30	BP/1734	11/1879	-	12/12/1904	
31	BP/1729	3/1880	11/9/1911	13/3/1928	Cut up 10/5/1928
32	BP/1730	11/1879	-	7/1926	Sold new to Millars 6/1879
33	BP/1731	6/1879	26/5/1911	8/4/1928	Cut up 16/4/1928
34	BP/1732	6/1879	16/3/1906	17/5/1929	Sold for scrap 8/1929
35	BP/1733	11/1879	-	1/1/1911	To C.R. NF7 (part
36	BP/1822	3/1880	-	1/1/1911	To C.R. NF4
37	BP/1823	9/1879	19/5/1905	3/1959	Cut up 13/1/1961
38	BP/2050	13/7/1881	-	3/3/1896	To Baxter & Saddler
39	BP/2051	2/7/1881	15/6/1904	17/1/1929	Cut up 23/1/1929
40	BP/2052	26/7/1881	26/9/1903	17/5/1929	Sold for scrap 8/1929
41	BP/2139	9/8/1882	-	1/1/1911	To C.R. NF7 (parts)
42	BP/2140	6/1882	-	17/5/1929	Sold for scrap 8/1929
43	BP/2141	9/6/1882	-	7/2/1896	To Baxter & Saddler
53	BP/1717	6/1883	-	12/1911	Contractor/C.R. NF5
54	BP/1721	3/1883	-	26/1/1912	Contractor/C.R. NF6
55	BP/1725	3/1883	20/1/1914	12/7/1928	Cut up 6/9/1928
56	BP/1718	10/1883	13/5/1912	3/1959	Original No. 22 (1878)

X Class   2-6-0

When the X class arrived aboard the ship *John Loughlin* they must have looked rather strange when compared to the neat and conservative English locomotives of the period. They were constructed by the Baldwin Locomotive Works, Philadelphia, U.S.A., and were typically North American in appearance with their diamond type spark arrestors, large cabs, large and ornate domes and sandboxes, bogie tenders, circular smokebox mounted number plates and high footplates.

All eight engines were allocated to the northern systems, Nos. 44 and 45 going to Port Wakefield, 46 and 47 to Port Pirie and 48 to 51 to Port Augusta. They were used to supplement the then current locomotive fleet working mainline trains inland from these ports.

X45 as supplied to the S.A.R. with the usual American style fittings.   (*S.A. Archives*)

X45 in final form with extended smokebox and copper capped chimney.
(Author's collection)

X47 was transferred to Port Augusta in 1883 and the two Port Wakefield locomotives were transferred to Port Pirie in 1884. With the bulk of the class now allocated to Port Augusta they occasionally worked through to Government Gums (Farina), mainly on cattle trains, but regularly worked south from Port Augusta and through the Pichi Richi Pass to Peterborough and Terowie.

In April 1886 No. 47 was sold to the construction department and was used during the construction of the extension of the Great Northern Railway to Oodnadatta. It returned to the S.A.R. afterwards and was reissued to traffic in 1891.

As more of the new Y class arrived at Port Augusta they released some of the X class for work elsewhere. In 1886 most of the class were transferred to Peterborough and used on construction trains on the Cockburn line. They were then employed on general goods traffic and worked right through to Broken Hill on ore trains until 1893 when the Silverton Tramway Company resumed its own train operations between Burns and Broken Hill.

No. 49 was sold to Millars on 29th December 1896 and sent to Western Australia for further service. It was later sold to Millars Timber and Trading Company and was finally scrapped in June 1943.

The viability of the early coal mines at Leigh Creek had been questionable for some time and in an effort to create more demand, therefore saving the mine from ultimate closure, the owners persuaded the S.A.R. to trial their coal in two of their locomotives. X48 and Y60 were fitted with extended smokeboxes during 1897 in an effort to improve combustion. Tests were carried out between Port Augusta and Hergott Springs. However, with the high ash content and increase in chimney cinder emissions the S.A.R. were not overly impressed and shelved any thoughts of burning Leigh Creek coal in their locomotives. The mine ceased production that year. Ironically it was to be Leigh Creek coal that provided most of the traffic over the line in the late 1940s and 50s.

Five of the class, Nos. 44, 46, 47, 50 and 51 were condemned in December 1904, followed by No. 45 in February 1905 and finally No. 48 in April 1907. This brought to a close the short lives of these distinctive little locomotives.

Introduced	:	1881	Heating Surface	:
Builder	:	Baldwin	Tubes	: 497.49sq ft.
Driving Wheel	:	3ft 2in.	Superheater	: -
Bogie Wheel	:	2ft 2in.	Firebox	: 65.62sq ft.
Weight in W.O.	:	39tons 1cwt. 2qtr.	Grate Area	: 14.57sq ft.
Max. Axle Load	:	6tons 9cwt 2qtr.	Boiler Pressure	: 130lb./sq in.
Length	:	42ft 8¼in.	Tractive Effort	: 11,005lb.
Water	:	1,300 gallons	Cylinders	: 2(O) 14½ x 18in.
Total	:	8	Coal	: 3tons 15¾ cwt.

No.	Bldr./No.	In Service	Condemned	Notes
44	Bdwn/5234	21/4/1881	12/12/1904	Issued to Port Wakefield
45	Bdwn/5237	3/3/1882	26/7/1905	Issued to Port Wakefield
46	Bdwn/5246	14/2/1882	12/12/1904	Issued to Port Pirie
47	Bdwn/5247	10/1/1882	12/12/1904	Issued to Port Pirie
48	Bdwn/5230	26/6/1881	10/4/1907	Issued to Port Augusta
49	Bdwn/5244	20/5/1882	29/12/1896	Issued to Port Augusta
50	Bdwn/5229	17/6/1882	12/12/1904	Issued to Port Augusta
51	Bdwn/5235	14/6/1882	12/12/1904	Issued to Port Augusta

Based on a broad gauge design this solitary locomotive was built for use on the narrow gauge and spent its life on the Northern Division.   *(Government of South Australia)*

K Class   0-6-4T

The K class are perhaps better known for their exploits on the broad gauge. The first batch entered traffic in 1879, primarily for working on the Kapunda to Morgan line. However, after about twelve months they were replaced and found employment in the Adelaide metropolitan area, with the occasional country turns. In all eighteen of the class were placed in traffic on the S.A.R. broad gauge system between 1879 and 1885. They were all built by Beyer Peacock & Co.

It seems rather odd that a solitary locomotive of the same type, built by Dubs & Co., should be purchased for the narrow gauge. One can only speculate that there were thoughts of using it as a prototype for short haul heavy goods work or alternatively for banking duties or shunting the heavy ore trains. At the time it was the most powerful locomotive on the narrow gauge, but despite the use of tank locomotives for main line work on other railways they had obvious limitations.

Perhaps the initial poor performance of the broad gauge K class and the imminent arrival of the first of the new Y class cut short any plans for further locomotives. Either way it was to be the sole representative of its type on the narrow gauge. It was also unusual in that it was the only inside cylindered locomotive on the narrow gauge.

K52's early history is not known, but by the time the roundhouse had been built at Peterborough it was gainfully employed as shunter and shed pilot. K52 and a T class would just fit on the 85 foot turntable. It was condemned in May 1938.

Introduced	:	1884	Heating Surface	:	
Builder	:	Dubs & Co.	Tubes	:	699.53sq ft.
Driving Wheel	:	3ft 6in.	Superheater	:	-
Bogie Wheel	:	2ft 3in.	Firebox	:	77.90sq ft.
Weight in W.O.	:	32tons 12cwt.	Grate Area	:	13.14sq ft.
Max.Axle Load	:	6ton 15cwt.	Boiler Pressure	:	130lb./sq in.
Length	:	30ft 10½in.	Tractive Effort	:	11,063lb.
Water	:	940 gallons	Cylinders	:	2(I) 14½ x 20in.
Total	:	1	Coal	:	1ton 2cwt. 3qtr.

No.	Bldr./No.	In Service	Condemned	Notes
52	Dubs/1784	25/1/1884	24/5/1938	Used for shunting, Peterborough

K52 at Peterborough. *(Author's collection)*

Y & Yx Classes

2-6-0

Words like 'sturdy', 'reliable' and 'workhorses' have been used to describe the S.A.R. Y class. These locomotives were the most numerous class ever to operate on the S.A.R., with no less than one hundred and twenty nine placed on the books. The design was also adopted by other railways in Australia, both government and private. The Western Australian Government Railways, Tasmanian Government Railways and the Commonwealth Railways all operated Y or Yx class locomotives while private railways such as the Silverton Tramway (N.S.W.), Broken Hill Proprietary Co., Whyalla (S.A.), the Emu Bay Railway (Tasmania) and of course the vast saw milling interests in Western Australia also found a home for them. In their early years they were also used by railway construction companies and then resold.

Y93 with early narrow smokebox and chimney.   *(S.A. Archives)*

They were very popular locomotives and despite their age a few were still working in the 1960s, with S.A.R. No. 97 still on the active list until the end of narrow gauge steam in January 1970.

Their design can be attributed to the English firm of Beyer Peacock & Co. and they were typical of products from their Gorton foundry. They were neat and tidy, of solid construction and basic in operation. The sloping cylinders, large centrally mounted steam dome and tapered copper top chimney were trade marks of the company and the era generally.

The Y class were introduced on the S.A.R. to replace the earlier smaller types and although of the same 2-6-0 wheel arrangement were much more powerful. The first of the class arrived in South Australia in 1885 and new locomotives continued to be supplied until 1898. By this time James Martin & Co. of Gawler had built a number of the class while the S.A.R's own workshops had contributed two locomotives. In fact, Y178 and Y179 were the first steam engines built at Islington workshops.

The Y class were immediately put to work on the most arduous of tasks, the Barrier ore traffic from Cockburn to Port Pirie and the long distance services between Port Augusta and Oodnadatta. As more of the class became available they were used extensively throughout the narrow gauge systems.

With the arrival of the T class, the conversion of the Western Division to broad gauge and the transfer of the Great Northern and Palmerston lines to the Commonwealth a number of the class were disposed of. The following table gives known movements of the various locomotives.

Abbreviations are as follows; C.R. = Commonwealth Railways, B.H.P. = Broken Hill Proprietary Co., W.A.J.F. = W.A. Jarrah Forrest Co. Ltd., V.C.C. = Victorian Construction Company, B.B. = Bunning Bros. W.A., T.G.R. = Tasmanian Government Railways, E.B.R. = Emu Bay Railway, W.A.G.F. = W.A. Goldfields Firewood Supply, M.T.T. = Millars Timber & Trading Co., W.A., K.T.C. = Kauri Timber Co., W.A.

S.A.R. No.	Sold to	Date	New No.	Withdrawn
38	C.R.	10/3/1944	NFB93	1952
61	B.H.P.	10/1926	61	1935
71	W.A.J.F.	22/4/1927	71	c1957
79	V.C.C.	3/9/1928		1943
86	V.C.C.	5/1/1928		
	B.B.	1944		3/1970
96	V.C.C.	3/9/1928		?
108	C.R.	6/4/1944	NFB94	-
	T.G.R.	3/1949	F2	7/8/1956
109	K.T.C.	7/6/1921	109	1961
116	C.R.	5/9/1941	NFB43	-
	T.G.R.	3/1949	F3	1/8/1962
117	C.R.	10/6/1944	NFB96	-
	T.G.R.	2/1949	F1	-
	E.B.R.	18/5/1956	19	23/7/1963
119	C.R.	9/2/1944	NFB90	c1955
121	C.R.	3/2/1944	NFB91	-
	T.G.R.	1949	For spare parts	
126	C.R.	5/2/1942	NFB47	7/1952
127	C.R.	1/2/1944	NFB92	1952
132	C.R.	29/3/1942	NFB49	23/10/1958
135	C.R.	29/10/1943	NFB88	Preserved
138	C.R.	5/2/1942	NFB48	-
	T.G.R.	5/1949	F4	2/5/1958
140	C.R.	21/8/1944	NFB97	c1955
153 1st	W.A.G.R.	6/1896	G126	?
154 1st	W.A.G.R.	6/1896	G128	?
154 2nd	C.R.	23/12/1943	NFB89	5/1951
155 1st	W.A.G.R.	6/1896	G127	?
156 1st	W.A.G.R.	6/1896	G129	-
	C.R.	14/8/1942	NFC66	-
	W.A.G.F.	6/1947		?
156 2nd	C.R.	25/9/1941	NFB46	-
	T.G.R.	1949	For spare parts	
157 1st	W.A.G.R.	6/1896	G131	-
	C.R.	11/1942	NGA76 1st	-
	C.R.	Renumbered	NFC74	-
	W.A.G.R.	9/1947	G131	-
	B.B.	c1960	Parts for Y109	
158 1st	M.T.T.	17/4/1896	69 Waroona	11/1957
159 1st	W.A.G.R.	6/1896	G130	?
160	C.R.	29/3/1942	NFB51	5/1951
166	C.R.	5/9/1941	NFB44	-
	T.G.R.	1949	For spare parts	
169	C.R.	5/5/1944	NFB95	4/1953
176	B.B.	12/8/1937	176	Preserved
178	C.R.	25/9/1941	NFB45	1948

Newly rebuilt Yx No. 169, Islington, 1906.   *(Government of South Australia)*

On the Commonwealth Railways some of the class were converted to burn oil.

As some locomotives were disposed of after a short period on the S.A.R. their numbers were reissued to their replacements. We have used the designation 1st and 2nd to differentiate between the two. The locomotives themselves were not identified as such!

The Y class required few modifications over the years. However, some of the class were to lose their copper capped chimneys for the plain stove pipe type, smokeboxes were extended and electric lighting was added from the late 1920s.

Fifty eight of the class were rebuilt with larger boilers with a Belpaire firebox and reclassified as Yx. This resulted in an increase in power of just over 25%.

No.	Date rebuilt to Yx	No.	Date rebuilt to Yx
38	14/4/1910	140	25/4/1913
43	15/6/1909	141	26/7/1923
49	2/11/1908	148	25/11/1912
108	30/10/1915	149	31/10/1913
110	25/11/1919	152	14/12/1915
111	3/4/1917	153 (2nd)	19/12/1907
112	2/6/1919	154 (2nd)	23/3/1910
113	28/7/1919	155 (2nd)	13/3/1916
114	20/9/1916	156 (2nd)	9/3/1910
115	24/8/1922	157 (2nd)	18/10/1907
116	16/11/1923	158 (2nd)	8/6/1909
117	1/9/1919	159 (2nd)	6/6/1913
118	5/10/1920	160	5/10/1916
119	4/9/1923	162	16/2/1906
121	27/7/1920	164	29/7/1907
122	20/8/1923	165	27/2/1907
123	24/4/1917	166	4/5/1909
124	7/11/1919	167	22/10/1906
125	16/5/1919	168	23/8/1906
126	15/8/1922	169	9/5/1906
127	3/8/1920	170	25/10/1912
128	10/4/1924	171	7/5/1907
129	19/3/1913	172	8/6/1907
132	5/5/1916	173	5/8/1913
133	24/1/1913	174	12/11/1908
135	4/4/1919	175	12/5/1910
136	11/8/1916	177	4/10/1913
137	28/6/1913	178	7/7/1910
138	2/11/1923	179	11/12/1916

In addition, two of the class, Nos. 86 and 176, were converted to Yx by Bunnings (W.A.) as late as 1958 and 1956 respectively. The rebuilding of the S.A.R. locomotives took place between 1906 and 1923.

Other minor modifications were made to these locomotives over the years including the altering of their baffle plates and spark arresters from 1938. From 1939 an additional washout plug was fitted to the smokebox tubeplate on the Yx group. Both Y and Yx tubeplates were altered from 1944 and their pilot (cow catcher) was redesigned.

Y class No. 98 at Naracoorte depot.   *(Unknown/Ron Stewien collection)*

The Westinghouse air compressor silencer was altered in 1945, while the fire hole door was modified and the water gauge mounting altered from 1947. Cow catchers were removed from 1953.

Some time prior to 1910 rails had been fitted on the top of their tenders to increase the coal capacity. Instructions were issued in 1930 regarding the coaling of Y, Yx and Z class tenders. One hundred baskets of coal was considered ample for any duties these engines may have undertaken, although one hundred and seventeen baskets would fill the tender to capacity. The original coal capacity for their tenders was 3tons 16cwt, but this was increased to 4tons 10cwt after the rails were fitted.

Two Y class, Nos. 70 and 76, were involved in the Walloway disaster of 1901. On the 16th November that year a southbound cattle train and a northbound special mixed goods collided head on just three hundred yards south of Walloway station, killing both firemen and injuring the two drivers. Evidently the southbound cattle train couldn't stop in the yard after descending the Walloway hills.

The Y class were very successful and although they were overshadowed by the larger T class they were still gainfully employed throughout the system. However, their numbers had reduced considerably by the mid 1940s.

In 1948 a survey of narrow gauge motive power and goods rolling stock was undertaken due to the proposed increase in Leigh Creek coal traffic. From this survey it was ascertained that there were still seventeen Y class and seven Yx class listed as trafficable. The locomotives concerned were; (Y) 58, 66, 67, 68, 76, 77, 82, 87, 91, 93, 95, 97, 98, 104, 134, 142, 151 and (Yx) 112, 115, 118, 122, 141, 162, 164.

Distribution of the survivors in June 1948 was as follows;

| | **Peterborough** | | **South East** | | **Port Lincoln** | |
	Allotted	On Div.	Allotted	On Div.	Allotted	On Div.
Y	9	6	8	7	-	-
Yx	2	2	-	-	5	5

The four missing Y class were to be found at Islington workshops; two were scheduled for repairs and then return to Peterborough, while the future of the other two was uncertain.

On the Peterborough Division the Y and Yx locomotives were relegated to shunting. Three were to be found at Peterborough, three at Terowie (included tippler working), two at Port Pirie and one at Cockburn. This allowed for one spare locomotive for servicing or overhaul.

By 1953 only six of the class were left on the Peterborough Division. Five were available for traffic with one normally under repair. Over the next ten years the class was to disappear from the South East and Port Lincoln, leaving only one survivor at Peterborough. This solitary representative was to remain in service for another seven years as shed pilot at Peterborough roundhouse. For this duty it was coupled to W class tender No. 19. However, during its last few years in service it was used on the mainline on a number of enthusiasts specials and for these trips it had its original tender and early bar type cow catcher replaced. The bar type cow catcher and also its copper top chimney were actually taken from Silverton Tramway locomotives which were at Terowie enroute to the scrap merchant.

At Peterborough Y97 acquired the nickname 'the rat', which was a term of endearment handed down from other smaller locomotives which were used as shed pilots. Y97 remained active until the end of narrow gauge steam in January 1970. The familiar sight of its smokebox protruding from one of the roundhouse bays, with smoke gently rolling out of the chimney, was a sight that welcomed many a visitor. It was last used on the mainline on 13th May 1970 on an Australian Railway Historical Society special train to Eurelia and return. It was transferred to the Mile End Railway Museum in September 1970. After eighty five years of faithful service the Y class era had finally come to an end.

Despite their large numbers the Y and Yx classes are poorly represented in preservation in their home territory. There are also no active examples of former S.A.R. locomotives of this type.

In South Australia only Y82 survives near the caravan park at Peterborough and Y97 is at the Port Dock Station Railway Museum. The only Yx to survive is No. 141 which was preserved at Port Lincoln in October 1963. It was transferred to the Pichi Richi Railway in 1983 and is currently stored at their Quorn depot.

In Western Australia former S.A.R. Y71 and Yx86 are preserved at the A.R.H.S. Railway Museum at Bassendean, while a third locomotive, Yx176, has been retained by Bunnings. A rather hybrid locomotive referred to as Y109 is preserved at the Manjimup Timber Museum. It is actually made up of parts from three locomotives, ex S.A.R. Y109, ex W.A.G.R. G131 and A7.

Of the locomotives sold to the Commonwealth, only NFB88 (formerly Yx135) has been preserved at Katherine, N.T.

The Silverton Tramway Company operated a fleet of Y class and three have been preserved. Y1 can be found at the Sulphide Street Station Museum in Broken Hill, Y11 at Penrose Park, Silverton and Y12 at Port Dock Station Railway Museum.

Although not mentioned in the following specifications it should be noted that in the early years there was a variation in the boiler pressures of the Y class. An early diagram gives a boiler pressure of 130lb./sq in., for a locomotive with a single rivetted boiler and 145lb./sq in. for double rivetted. This lower pressure would also reduce the tractive effort.

Introduced	:	1885,	Heating Surface	:	
	:	Yx 1906	Tubes	:	708.46sq ft.
Builders	:	BP, JM & Isl.		:	Yx 730 sq ft.
Driving Wheel	:	3ft 3in.	Superheater	:	-
Bogie Wheel	:	2ft 0in.	Firebox	:	69.48sq ft.
Weight in W.O.	:	47tons 15cwt.			Yx 76.2sq ft.
		Yx 49tons 19cwt.	Grate Area	:	13.67sq ft.
Max. Axle Load	:	7tons 9cwt.	Boiler Pressure	:	145lb./sq in.
Length	:	39ft 3 1/8in.			Yx 185lb./sq in.
Water	:	1,600 gallons	Tractive Effort	:	13,289lb.
Coal	:	4tons 10cwt.			Yx 16,955lb.
Total	:	129	Cylinders	:	2(O) 14½ x 20in.

No.	Bldr./No.	In Service	Condemned	Notes
22	JM/14	8/2/1892	12/8/1929	Originally numbered Y195
38	JM/164	27/10/1897	10/3/1944	Yx. To C.R. as NFB93
43	JM/165	12/11/1897	25/7/1930	Yx.
49	JM/166	13/11/1897	21/3/1928	Yx
57	BP/2478	12/10/1885	17/5/1929	At Port Lincoln
58	BP/2536	12/10/1885	18/7/1958	At Port Lincoln
59	BP/2537	9/9/1885	6/1936	
60	BP/2539	9/9/1885	6/1936	To South East 1929
61	BP/2538	29/9/1885	10/1926	Sold to B.H.P.
62	BP/2540	29/9/1885	1/12/1936	
63	BP/2541	29/9/1885	7/11/1939	To Port Lincoln 1923
64	BP/2755	17/8/1886	12/3/1936	
65	BP/2756	23/8/1886	1/12/1934	To Port Lincoln 1922
66	BP/2757	28/8/1886	23/1/1956	Scrapped 3/1956
67	BP/2758	2/9/1886	4/12/1957	To South East 1932
68	BP/2759	13/9/1886	8/6/1956	To South East 1928
69	BP/2760	15/9/1886	1/12/1934	To Port Lincoln 1918
70	BP/2761	6/10/1886	12/8/1929	To Port Lincoln 1924
71	BP/2762	30/9/1886	24/4/1927	Preserved in W.A.
72	BP/2763	22/10/1886	1/12/1936	Withdrawn 1929
73	BP/2764	24/11/1886	1/12/1936	Withdrawn 1930
74	BP/2765	23/11/1886	1/12/1936	Withdrawn 1930
75	BP/2766	19/11/1886	1/12/1934	To Port Lincoln 1924
76	BP/2767	6/12/1886	1/1956	
77	BP/2768	14/12/1886	4/9/1962	Used in South East
78	BP/2769	22/12/1886	1/12/1936	
79	BP/2770	4/1/1887	1928	Sold to V.C.C.
80	BP/2907	25/4/1888	27/2/1940	To Port Lincoln 1918
81	BP/2908	30/4/1888	1/12/1934	To Port Lincoln 1922
82	BP/2909	30/4/1888	14/4/1960	Preserved at Peterborough

Above: T203 at Islington workshops, 13th September 1934. This locomotive had been specially prepared in readiness to haul the Royal Train the following month and was meticulously cleaned with all the brasswork shining. Its modifications from original include the high sided tender, first extension of the smokebox and electric lighting.

(Government of South Australia)

Below: Islington built Y class No. 179 being prepared for its official photograph, 1898. Y178 and Y179 were the first two steam locomotives to be built at Islington workshops and it was therefore a proud moment for the South Australian Railways. The white sheeting behind the locomotive was commonly used to conceal any background objects that would cause distraction in the photograph.

(Government of South Australia)

179
S A R

83	BP/2910	9/8/1888	6/1936	Withdrawn 1930
84	BP/2911	9/8/1888	1/12/1936	Withdrawn 1930
85	BP/2912	9/8/1888	1/12/1936	Withdrawn 1930
86	BP/2913	16/7/1888	5/1/1928	Preserved in W.A.
87	BP/2914	16/7/1888	4/12/1957	Used in South East
88	BP/2915	16/7/1888	1/12/1936	Withdrawn 1930
89	BP/2690	21/3/1888	6/1936	New 2/1886 to C & E. Millar
90	BP/2973	7/11/1888	1/12/1936	Purchased new from S.T.C.
91	BP/2974	7/11/1888	23/1/1956	Purchased new from S.T.C.
92	BP/3142	16/1/1890	6/1936	Withdrawn 1931
93	BP/3143	20/1/1890	8/6/1956	Used in South East
94	BP/3144	29/1/1890	1/12/1934	To Port Lincoln 1924
95	BP/3145	29/1/1890	23/1/1956	Used in South East
96	BP/3146	27/2/1890	3/9/1928	Sold to V.C.C.
97	BP/3147	27/2/1890	14/5/1970	Preserved at Port Dock Museum
98	BP/3148	27/2/1890	4/9/1962	Used in South East
99	BP/3149	18/2/1890	1/12/1934	To Port Lincoln 1918
100	BP/3150	18/2/1890	5/1928	Used in South East
101	BP/3151	18/2/1890	1/12/1936	Withdrawn 1931
102	BP/3152	2/4/1890	12/3/1936	
103	BP/3153	2/4/1890	7/11/1939	To Port Lincoln 1923
104	BP/3154	2/4/1890	4/12/1957	Used in South East
105	BP/3155	2/4/1890	1/12/1936	
106	BP/2689	16/9/1890	7/1926	New 1885 to C. & E. Millar
108	JM/7	30/5/1890	6/4/1944	Yx. To C.R. as NFB94
109	JM/8	30/5/1890	7/6/1921	Preserved in W.A.
110	JM/9	7/11/1890	21/3/1928	Yx. Scrapped 17/12/1928
111	JM/10	11/12/1890	21/3/1928	Yx.
112	JM/11	17/12/1890	11/1/1963	Yx. To Port Lincoln 1946
113	JM/12	19/12/1890	22/9/1936	Yx. Withdrawn 1930
114	JM/13	25/2/1891	22/9/1936	Yx.
115	JM/27	2/4/1892	11/1/1963	Yx. To Port Lincoln 1933
116	JM/15	19/3/1891	5/9/1941	Yx. To C.R. as NFB43
117	JM/28	29/4/1892	10/6/1944	Yx. To C.R. as NFB96
118	JM/17	5/5/1891	11/1/1963	Yx. To Port Lincoln 1956
119	JM/18	12/5/1891	9/2/1944	Yx. To C.R. as NFB90
120	JM/29	18/5/1892	2/7/1935	Used in South East
121	JM/20	13/7/1891	3/2/1944	Yx. To C.R. as NFB91
122	JM/21	11/8/1891	23/8/1963	Yx. To Port Lincoln 1933
123	JM/22	24/8/1891	22/9/1936	Yx. Withdrawn 1930
124	JM/23	3/9/1891	2/7/1935	Yx.
125	JM/24	16/9/1891	22/9/1936	Yx. To Port Lincoln 1925
126	JM/25	24/9/1891	5/2/1942	Yx. To C.R. as NFB47
127	JM/26	6/10/1891	1/2/1944	Yx. To C.R. as NFB92
128	JM/30	26/5/1892	2/7/1935	Yx.
129	JM/31	7/6/1892	2/7/1935	Yx.
130	JM/32	22/6/1892	1/12/1936	Withdrawn 1930
131	JM/33	30/6/1892	1/12/1936	Withdrawn 1930
132	JM/34	23/7/1892	29/3/1942	Yx. To C.R. as NFB49
133	JM/35	4/8/1892	22/9/1936	Yx. Withdrawn 1929
134	JM/36	13/9/1892	23/1/1956	Used in South East
135	JM/37	20/9/1892	29/10/1943	Yx. C.R. NFB88. Preserved
136	JM/38	12/10/1892	22/9/1936	Yx.
137	JM/39	20/10/1892	22/9/1936	Yx.

138	JM/40	7/11/1892	5/2/1942	Yx. To C.R. as NFB48
139	JM/41	12/11/1892	12/3/1936	Withdrawn 1930
140	JM/42	1/12/1892	21/8/1944	Yx. To C.R. as NFB97
141	JM/43	15/12/1892	23/8/1963	Yx. Preserved at Quorn
142	JM/44	22/12/1892	27/12/1956	Scrapped 1961
147	JM/77	23/3/1894	7/1926	Scrapped 1927
148	JM/78	3/4/1894	22/9/1936	Yx. Withdrawn 1930
149	JM/79	10/4/1894	22/9/1936	Yx.
150	JM/80	25/4/1894	12/3/1936	Withdrawn 1930
151	JM/81	4/5/1894	27/12/1956	Scrapped 1961
152	JM/82	19/6/1894	22/9/1936	Yx.
153	(1)JM/113	11/7/1895	31/3/1896	To W.A.G.R. as G126
153	(2)JM/157	17/6/1897	7/3/1936	Yx. Withdrawn 1930
154	(1)JM/114	18/7/1895	8/4/1896	To W.A.G.R. as G128
154	(2)JM/158	24/6/1897	23/12/1943	Yx. To C.R. as NFB89
155	(1)JM/115	31/7/1895	3/4/1896	To W.A.G.R. as G127
155	(2)JM/159	17/7/1897	2/7/1935	Yx.
156	(1)JM/126	6/12/1895	3/4/1896	To W.A.G.R. as G129
156	(2)JM/160	7/9/1897	25/9/1941	Yx. To C.R. as NFB46
157	(1)JM/127	23/12/1895	13/4/1896	To W.A.G.R. as G131
157	(2)JM/161	30/9/1897	22/7/1936	Yx.
158	(1)JM/128	21/1/1896	17/4/1896	Returned to JM, defective boiler
158	(2)JM/162	18/10/1897	21/3/1928	Yx.
159	(1)JM/129	25/1/1896	2/4/1896	To W.A.G.R. as G130
159	(2)JM/163	18/10/1897	12/3/1936	Yx. Withdrawn 1930
160	JM/141	31/10/1896	29/3/1942	Yx. To C.R. as NFB51
161	JM/131	11/8/1896	1/10/1929	Scrapped 1929
162	JM/139	25/9/1896	11/1/1963	Yx. Used on all divisions

Former S.A.R. Y class No. 86 was converted to a Yx by its last owners, Bunning Bros (W.A.). It is now preserved at Bassendean Railway Museum, 3rd August 1991.

(Steve McNicol)

163	JM/140	28/10/1896	17/5/1929	To Port Lincoln 1920
164	JM/142	7/12/1896	18/7/1958	Yx. To Port Lincoln 1926
165	JM/138	7/9/1896	21/3/1928	Yx. Scrapped 1930
166	JM/143	17/12/1896	5/9/1941	Yx. To C.R. as NFB44
167	JM/144	1/3/1897	1/12/1936	Yx. Withdrawn 1930
168	JM/145	15/3/1897	22/9/1936	Yx. Withdrawn 1930
169	JM/146	31/3/1897	5/5/1944	Yx. To C.R. as NFB95
170	JM/147	17/4/1897	22/9/1936	Yx. Withdrawn 1930
171	JM/148	28/4/1897	22/9/1936	Yx. Withdrawn 1928
172	JM/149	19/5/1897	2/7/1935	Yx.
173	JM/150	15/6/1897	23/1/1935	Yx. To Port Lincoln 1927
174	JM/167	9/12/1897	21/3/1928	Yx.
175	JM/177	29/9/1898	22/9/1936	Yx.
176	JM/178	8/11/1898	1/12/1936	Preserved in W.A. as Yx176
177	JM/170	16/12/1897	22/9/1936	Yx.
178	SAR/2	9/9/1898	25/9/1941	Yx. To C.R. as NFB45
179	SAR/1	29/9/1898	22/9/1936	Yx.
195	see Y22			Renumbered Y22 10/1895

The last Y class in S.A.R. service was No. 97. It ended its years as shed pilot at Peterborough, but was occasionally used on enthusiast specials prior to the end of steam. Y97 is pictured below in its final form while working an enthusiasts' special in the late 1960s. The copper cap chimney and bar type cow catcher were fittings from an earlier era.
(David Goscombe)

No other locomotive has left its mark on the narrow gauge more than the T class. These ungainly looking machines were greatly modified over the years, but were the faithful workhorses of the narrow gauge until the end. They were uniquely South Australian, having been designed by the South Australian Railways at Islington, but they inherited many features from the earlier Y class.

The story of the T class began back in the 1890s when it became obvious the Y class 2-6-0s were struggling with the ever increasing Barrier ore traffic. This traffic had doubled between 1892 and 1900, which taxed these small locomotives to the limit. A new larger locomotive would remove the need for double heading which would also reduce operating costs. The design team at Islington produced, what was in its time, a large handsome locomotive with a much greater hauling capacity. The increase in boiler size was matched with an extra set of driving wheels and a four wheel bogie instead of the single truck of the Y class.

In November 1900 the materials required for the pattern engine were ordered from England. On their arrival in South Australia work commenced and on Thursday the 16th February 1903 T class No. 180 entered service on what was then referred to as the Northern Division (later known as the Peterborough Division). It proved very successful and was capable of hauling 50% more than a Y class.

In March 1902, almost twelve months before 180 entered traffic, the first tender was called for two additional T class. James Martin & Co., were the successful bidders and Nos. 181 and 182 entered traffic in July and August 1904 respectively. In 1907 they were followed by three more Islington built locomotives (44 to 46). James Martin then built the next thirty two locomotives between 1909 and 1913. The Queensland firm of Walkers Ltd. was successful with later tenders and provided another forty locomotives between 1914 and 1917. The class total had reached seventy eight.

During 1923 T class No. 225 was fitted with a superheater and used on trials over the Peterborough Division. A written report was tabled in May 1923 with the result being that the rest of the class were fitted with superheaters between June 1925 and May 1939. When built the smokebox door was situated directly above the front of the cylinders. However, when superheated the smokebox was extended forwards and a short horizontal extension fitted to the footplate. They retained their original chimney until 1933 when the ornate 'copper cap' and brass numbers started disappearing, being replaced by rather plain stove pipes. Initially the chimneys were sleeved and some locomotives appeared minus copper top, but still with the moulded base.

From 1946 most of the class received a 'Cyclone' front end and spark arrester for burning the poorer quality Leigh Creek coal. Spark arrester screens were actually suggested back in 1938, as well as smoke deflectors, but one questions the effectiveness of the latter (in lifting smoke clear of the cab) due to the low speeds on the narrow gauge. With the 'Cyclone' front end came the second smokebox extension. Most of the locomotives were converted in Peterborough roundhouse, in the centre bays. During 1947 and 1949 further minor modifications were made to the exhaust pipe nozzle.

During 1949 No. 258 was selected to test cement firebricks and a copper alloy burner nozzle. Other tests were carried out with T class, including the fitting of a mechanical lubricator to one of the class in 1948. Silicone manganese steel springs were also considered from around 1943 and No. 253 was selected for trials during 1947.

Pictured in the late 1920s No. 50 has received few modifications. Electric lighting and a steel plate attached to the cow catcher are noticeable. (Unknown/Ron Stewien collection)

Instructions were issued during April 1947 to loco foremen at the various narrow gauge depots to mix two parts Newcastle coal with one part Leigh Creek coal. A year later this was altered to three parts Newcastle to one part Leigh Creek.

When quality coal from the Newcastle area became harder to acquire some of the locomotives were fitted out as oil burners, or oil/coal burners. The latter sprayed oil onto Leigh Creek coal. These modifications were mainly made at Peterborough. Unfortunately an official list is not available, but the locomotives concerned were believed to include; 44, 181, 186, 199, 206, 211, 238, 244, 255 and 257. 44, 199 and 211 were dual oil/coal burners and were frequently used on the Quorn to Hawker line. The conversions took place from 1949 and included the fitting of a heater for the oil. When cold the oil thickened and became hard to pump. To overcome this steam from the boiler passed through heating coils in the tank and then escaped through an exhaust pipe on the tender.

From the 1930s their tenders were systematically extended to increase coal capacity from six to eight tons. This also made it easier in later years to place the oil tanks on top of the higher sided tenders. Tender feed valves were altered around 1945. From 1948 numbers were painted on the back of T class tenders.

The steeper grades on the Peterborough Division, coupled with the Ts' tendency to slip due to their light axle load, resulted in lead adhesion blocks being fitted on the footplate to help overcome this problem. They were added in the late 1920s and weighed 3 tons 7cwt. This increased their adhesion factor from 3.14 to 3.52. During 1942 No. 202 had its weights removed and was tested on the Peterborough Division, apparently with little success as the weights were to remain with the class until their demise. The projecting securing bolts for the lead blocks were removed from 1946.

156

There were other minor modifications made such as the replacement of the original bar frame cow catcher with a solid steel pressed plate, boiler blowdown mufflers were fitted from 1938, auto couplers were fitted to some tenders from 1963, No. 23 was temporarily fitted with a chime whistle late in its life, steam generators were fitted atop the smokebox during the 1920s to power the electric headlights and speed recorders were fitted to locomotives used on the *Broken Hill Express*. The first official reference to speed recorders was found in 1937, but their actual fitting dates are not known.

From 1956 T class coupling rod bushes were altered to increase the clearance between the wheel and pin. Large power superheater elements were fitted to the surviving T class when required from 1962.

With a shortage of motive power in Tasmania six T class were purchased from the South Australian Railways during 1920/21. Nos. 219, 222, 223, 230, 235 and 237 were shipped to Tasmania and after conversion to Vacuum brake were all placed in traffic by the end of 1921. They retained their S.A.R. numbers.

T.G.R. modifications over the years included superheating of their boilers between 1927 and 1931, while they were fitted with electric headlights from 1930. The first was withdrawn in May 1957 and all six were out of traffic by September 1961. They were cut up by August 1963, but a few tenders survived. One is currently stored at Drysdale (Victoria) on the Bellarine Peninsula Railway. It is interesting in that their tenders were not modified like those on the mainland.

No.	Sold to T.G.R.	In Service T.G.R.	Superheated	Written off
219	11/1920	3/3/1921	26/9/1931	16/8/1957
222	8/1921	1921	15/8/1928	26/4/1960
223	8/1921	1921	26/12/1929	2/5/1958
230	8/1921	1921	23/4/1931	17/9/1958
235	11/1920	3/3/1921	10/10/1927	26/8/1963
237	8/1921	1921	30/9/1930	26/4/1960

During 1922/23 five T class were converted to broad gauge (reclassified Tx) for working mainly over the lightly laid Murraylands lines. They were based at Tailem Bend and used on goods and mixed traffic duties. With their small wheels and light axle load they were suitable for this type of branchline work. All five had returned to the narrow gauge by the end of 1949.

T class	Tx No.	Date Converted	Superheated	Back to N.G.
183	276	27/11/1922	25/8/1932	3/10/1949
199	277	27/3/1923	20/9/1933	6/4/1949
252	278	24/4/1923	18/12/1931	3/5/1949
243	279	21/6/1923	4/6/1935	11/10/1949
220	280	20/7/1923	11/5/1932	20/4/1949

In the early 1920s the South Australian Railways Commissioner had looked at the possibility of linking the Port Lincoln Division to the Peterborough Division, but there was just not enough traffic to justify the expense. However, he did have the Port Lincoln Division relaid to take the heavier T class to help improve train running efficiency. The first one was transferred to Port Lincoln in 1924 and others soon followed. No less than twenty four of the class were known to have spent time working on the Eyre Peninsula. Others may have gone to Port Lincoln, but unfortunately records are not complete.

The following lists known T class movements to and from Port Lincoln.

No.	Arrived	Departed	No.	Arrived	Departed
23	unknown	about 1960	212	6/1929	2/1942
45	7/11/1934	scrapped		11/1946	scrapped
46	3/1925	2/1942	214	2/1958	scrapped
48	9/12/1960	scrapped	216	25/2/1925	scrapped
50	6/1935	5/1942	217	12/12/1960	scrapped
	2/1946	2/1962	229	8/9/1928	scrapped
180	11/1952	scrapped	231	21/11/1924	scrapped
185	6/1956	18/11/1963	234	1945	scrapped
197	8/11/1957	scrapped	238	9/9/1961	scrapped
203	5/1956	scrapped	241	18/8/1961	scrapped
207	12/1956	scrapped	243	12/8/1952	1962
209	5/1/1925	scrapped	246	29/10/1946	scrapped
210	12/1956	scrapped	256	3/11/1934	2/1942

Minor variations could be seen on Port Lincoln Division T class, namely a larger rail car style headlight mounted on the tender and distinctive 'banjo' type sand boxes. Only coal burners were used on the division and the lead adhesion blocks were not required either. However, if locomotives returned to Peterborough the adhesion blocks were fitted and all but No. 185 had the 'banjo' type sand boxes removed and the traditional ones refitted.

The Port Lincoln Division also saw the last T class without the second smokebox extension. 212 was actually withdrawn from traffic without ever having received this modification and was cut up at Port Lincoln in 1969.

The last T class in service on the division were Nos. 45, 48, 209, 214, 234 and 241. No. 45 hauled the last mainline train to Kapinnie on 1st May 1969, although shunting continued a little longer.

Formerly the haven of the small W and Y classes the lightly laid South East Division had to wait until 1935 before the first T class was transferred. A number of T class worked on the division, including the following; 24, 44, 46, 47, 51, 185, 197, 201, 203, 208, 225, 232, 236, 241 and 249.

With gauge widening in the 1950s the Ts were transferred to either Peterborough or Port Lincoln. The last of the class to work on the division was No. 197, which was transferred to Port Lincoln on 8th November 1957.

The Second World War put a great strain on the Central Australia Railway with numerous military supply trains being run from Terowie to Alice Springs. The Commonwealth Railways used T class to supplement their locomotive fleet.

During 1942 four locomotives were sold to the Commonwealth Railways and were classified NMA. They were renumbered NMA 50, 52, 53 and 54 and were originally T class Nos. 46, 212, 256 and 50, although it is believed only two actually received their new identity. All four locomotives came from the Port Lincoln Division.

Later arrangements were made to hire T class from the S.A.R. and the NMAs were returned. Hired T class could be easily distinguished by the letters C.R. or T painted on the buffer beams.

Opposite: T252 and T257 at Quorn locomotive depot in the early 1950s.   *(Ron Stewien)*

158

As from 15th September 1944, military service traffic on the C.A.R. was limited to personnel and mechanical transport to and from Alice Springs and other parts of Northern Territory. A maximum of nine trains a week were required instead of the previous average of twenty one. The Commonwealth was paying £3 a day for each T class allocated to the C.A.R. pool so the reduction in trains meant the number of T class could also be reduced.

The following T class were amongst those believed to have been used on the C.A.R. during the early 1940s; 46, 47, 50, 51, 180, 182, 184, 185, 197, 198, 200, 201, 202, 204, 206, 207, 210, 211, 212, 214, 217, 218, 224. 226, 228, 239, 240, 242, 244, 245, 246, 247, 248, 249, 250, 253, 256 and 258. Unfortunately they were usually in poor condition when they returned to Peterborough and considerable maintenance was necessary.

The end of military traffic did not mean the end of T class working for the Commonwealth. Leigh Creek coal traffic, from the railhead at Telford, was to increase in the late 1940s. Between June and November 1948 the weekly tonnages were gradually increased from 5,200 tons to 8,000. All of this coal had to be transhipped through the Terowie coal tippler before it could be brought down to the power station at Osborne. To handle the traffic eighteen T class were allocated solely for Telford to Terowie coal traffic. The Commonwealth was still using its poorly maintained fleet of NM class on the coal traffic between Telford and Port Augusta and therefore had no spare locomotives it could pool for the extra Adelaide coal traffic.

Double heading of T class commenced in July 1948. Their trains weighed up to 660 tons and were around 1,000 feet long. After regular coal traffic ceased in 1956 a solitary T class was still used by the Commonwealth on the mixed goods from Quorn to Hawker. It would work from Peterborough on the Quorn goods and then return afterwards. This lasted until 6th January 1970.

During the mid 1960s a large number of T class were parked at Terowie and Peterborough. Some had been withdrawn from service after dieselisation of mainline services, but on 30th October 1967 they were put back on the books until the locomotive requirements were known for the changeover to standard gauge. This also meant an upsurge in steam workings while the diesels were being converted to standard gauge. Many parts from stored locomotives were used to keep the remaining engines in service. Two locomotives, 23 and 255, were actually condemned, but had been put back into service by July 1969.

T class in use on the Peterborough Division during July 1969 were; 23, 181, 185, 198, 199, 200, 206, 211, 218, 224, 240, 243, 244, 245, 251, 253, 255, 256 and 257. Of these, three were based at Port Pirie, two at Gladstone, two at Terowie and one at Cockburn. 45, 209, 234 and 241 were serviceable at Port Lincoln, with No. 48 at Thevenard. 24, 44, 50, 51, 182, 183, 186, 202, 220, 225, 228, 239, 242, 248, 250 and 258 were either stored or parked at Peterborough, while 46, 184, 204, 208, 213, 226, 227, 232, 236, 247, 249 and 252 were at Terowie.

The end for the class on the Peterborough Division came in January 1970. The last locomotives used on main line workings were Nos. 44, 181, 185, 186, 199, 200, 206, 211, 224, 240, 243, 244, 251, 253, 255 and 257. A few others in poor condition were used for shunting.

As I have already stated no other locomotive has left its mark or served the narrow gauge as well as the T class. Even in their twilight years they were regular performers and right up until the end of steam they carried out their tasks well. The sight of one of these locomotives pounding up Walloway, Gumbowie, Belalie or Yandiah banks will never be forgotten.

Luckily a few of the class have been preserved, but unfortunately none are active at the time of writing. Although No. 251, on the Bellarine Peninsula Railway, did work until recently it is now awaiting repairs. Possibly one of the saddest things to happen to a T class was when No. 200 was transferred to Islington for private preservation. The sale fell through and a mechanically sound locomotive was cut up.

Those preserved are; 181 at the Sulphide Street Station Museum in Broken Hill, 186 is on the Pichi Richi Railway at Quorn, 199 is in Peterborough and is currently being restored by Steamtown, 224 is in the National Trust museum at Millicent, 251 is at Queenscliff (Vic) on the Bellarine Peninsula Railway and 253 is preserved at Port Dock Station Railway Museum, Port Adelaide.

Introduced	:	1903	Heating Surface	:	
Builder	:	S.A.R. Isl.	Tubes	:	665sq ft.
		James Martin	Superheater	:	136sq ft.
		Walkers Ltd.	Firebox	:	109sq ft.
Driving Wheel	:	3ft 7in.	Grate Area	:	17.3sq ft.
Bogie Wheel	:	2ft 6in.	Boiler Pressure	:	185lb/sq in.
Weight in W.O.	:	78tons 8cwt.	Tractive Effort	:	21,904lb.
Max. Axle Load	:	9tons 1cwt.	Cylinders	:	2(O) 16½ x 22in.
Length	:	54ft 0in.	Fuel Coal	:	8tons
Water	:	2,418 gallons	Oil	:	1,050 gallons
Total	:	78	Oil/Coal	:	1,050gal/3tons

No.	Bldr./No.	In Service	Condemned	Notes
23	JM/189	23/2/1909	1/5/1970	300 class whistle fitted
24	JM/190	30/3/1909	12/8/1969	Stored Terowie 4/1969
44	Isl/5	20/3/1907	18/5/1970	Left Port Pirie 5/1/70
45	Isl/6	16/4/1907	22/6/1970	Last main line T Port Lincoln
46	Isl/7	26/3/1907	12/8/1969	Worked on all n.g. divisions
47	JM/191	1/5/1909	17/6/1959	Cut up Islington 8/1961
48	JM/192	5/6/1909	22/6/1970	Cut up Port Lincoln
50	Jm/193	2/7/1909	12/8/1969	Stored Peterborough 7/1969
51	JM/194	5/8/1909	1/5/1970	Stored Peterborough 7/1969
180	Isl/4	16/2/1903	7/9/1967	Pattern T class
181	JM/182	7/71904	9/1/1970	Preserved at Broken Hill
182	JM/183	8/8/1904	12/8/1969	Stored complete Peterborough
183	JM/195	28/8/1909	12/8/1969	Auto couplers fitted 1963
184	JM/196	27/9/1909	12/8/1969	Stored Terowie 7/1969
185	JM/197	5/11/1909	1/5/1970	Worked on all n.g. divisions
186	JM/198	9/12/1909	18/5/1970	Preserved at Quorn
197	JM/199	2/12/1911	9/7/1964	Last T in South East
198	JM/200	26/1/1912	1/5/1970	Shunter Peterborough 10/1969
199	JM/201	4/3/1912	1/5/1970	Preserved at Peterborough
200	JM/202	29/4/1912	1/5/1970	Cut up Islington 14/10/1972
201	JM/203	5/6/1912	17/6/1959	Cut up Islington 8/1961
202	JM/204	17/7/1912	1/5/1970	Stored at Peterborough 7/1969
203	JM/205	23/8/1912	2/2/1967	Cut up Port Lincoln
204	JM/206	30/9/1912	12/8/1969	Stored Terowie 4/1969
205	JM/207	30/10/1912	17/6/1959	Cut up Islington 8/1961

206	JM/208	2/12/1912	1/5/1970	Auto couplers fitted 1963
207	JM/209	2/1/1913	31/10/1968	Cut up Port Lincoln
208	JM/210	10/3/1913	12/8/1969	Stored Terowie 4/1969
209	JM/211	9/4/1913	22/6/1970	Cut up Port Lincoln
210	JM/212	13/5/1913	18/9/1967	Cut up Port Lincoln
211	JM/213	24/6/1913	1/5/1970	Last used on Quorn line
212	JM/214	14/7/1913	28/10/1966	Last with non extended smokebox
213	JM/215	8/8/1913	12/8/1969	Stored Terowie 4/1969
214	JM/216	3/9/1913	22/6/1970	Cut up Port Lincoln
215	JM/217	8/10/1913	17/6/1959	Cut up Islington 8/1961
216	JM/218	3/11/1913	28/10/1966	Rolled over at Karkarook 1964
217	JM/219	28/11/1913	31/10/1968	Cut up at Port Lincoln
218	JM/220	22/12/1913	12/8/1969	Accident with NM, Farina, 1943
219	Wlkr/219	13/5/1914	11/1920	Condemned 16/8/1957 T.G.R.
220	Wlkr/220	22/6/1914	12/8/1969	Stored Peterborough
221	Wlkr/221	27/5/1914	16/7/1963	Cut up Islington 2/10/1964
222	Wlkr/222	19/5/1914	8/1921	Condemned 26/4/1960 T.G.R.
223	Wlkr/223	9/6/1914	8/1921	Condemned 2/5/1958 T.G.R.
224	Wlkr/224	2/6/1914	1/5/1970	Preserved Millicent 21/2/1972
225	Wlkr/225	9/7/1914	1/5/1970	Stored Peterborough 7/1969
226	Wlkr/226	15/7/1914	12/8/1969	Accident with NM24, Copley 1944
227	Wlkr/227	21/7/1914	12/8/1969	Stored Terowie 4/1969
228	Wlkr/228	23/7/1914	1/5/1970	Auto couplers fitted 1963
229	Wlkr/229	4/8/1914	2/2/1967	Cut up Port Lincoln 4/1969
230	Wlkr/230	11/8/1914	8/1921	Condemned 17/9/1958 T.G.R.
231	Wlkr/231	30/7/1914	9/7/1964	Cut up at Port Lincoln
232	Wlkr/232	24/8/1914	12/8/1969	Stored Terowie 4/1969
233	Wlkr/233	28/8/1914	9/7/1964	Cut up 17/10/1964
234	Wlkr/234	3/9/1914	22/6/1970	Cut up Port Lincoln
235	Wlkr/235	8/9/1914	11/1920	Condemned 26/8/1963 T.G.R.
236	Wlkr/236	14/9/1914	12/8/1969	Stored Terowie 4/1969
237	Wlkr/237	5/10/1914	8/1921	Condemned 26/4/1960 T.G.R.
238	Wlkr/238	12/10/1914	31/10/1968	Cut up Port Lincoln
239	Wlkr/264	9/11/1916	1/5/1970	Stored Peterborough 7/1969
240	Wlkr/265	15/11/1916	1/5/1970	Last used on Wilmington line
241	Wlkr/266	22/11/1916	22/6/1970	Cut up Port Lincoln
242	Wlkr/267	27/11/1916	12/8/1969	Stored at Peterborough
243	Wlkr/268	4/12/1916	1/5/1970	Worked into Broken Hill 12/10/1969
244	Wlkr/269	11/12/1916	1/5/1970	Last n.g. shunter Port Pirie
245	Wlkr/270	18/12/1916	12/8/1969	In use Peterborough 7/1969
246	Wlkr/271	21/12/1916	31/10/1968	Cut up Port Lincoln
247	Wlkr/272	1/3/1917	12/8/1969	Stored Terowie 7/1969
248	Wlkr/273	8/3/1917	12/8/1969	Stored Peterborough 7/1969
249	Wlkr/274	14/3/1917	12/8/1969	Stored Terowie 7/1969
250	Wlkr/275	22/3/1917	12/8/1969	Stored Peterborough 7/1969
251	Wlkr/276	5/4/1917	1/5/1970	Preserved Queenscliff (Vic.)
252	Wlkr/277	20/4/1917	12/8/1969	Auto couplers fitted 1963
253	Wlkr/278	8/8/1917	1/5/1970	Preserved Port Adelaide
254	Wlkr/279	16/8/1917	17/6/1959	Cut up Islington 8/1961
255	Wlkr/280	23/8/1917	1/5/1970	Still in use 12/1969
256	Wlkr/281	28/8/1917	1/5/1970	In use Peterborough 7/1969
257	Wlkr/282	4/9/1917	1/5/1970	Still in use 12/1969
258	Wlkr/283	7/9/1917	12/8/1969	Stored Peterborough

T181 is one of six preserved T class. It can be found at the Sulphide Street Station Museum, Broken Hill where it was photographed on 18th August 1992.   (Steve McNicol)

No. 107 0-4-0ST

Between 1884 and 1891 a total of eight small 0-4-0 saddle tank locomotives were imported from the Baldwin Locomotive Works of Philadelphia U.S.A., by the Melbourne based firm of Newell & Co. They were designated as class 4-10½C, a standard Baldwin industrial locomotive type.

They were quite distinctive little engines with a spacious wooden cab, a large boiler mounted sandbox and large oil headlamps. They were typically North American in design with Stephensons valve gear and horizontal cylinders with steam chests on the top.

The first arrivals went to the Melbourne Harbour Trust for use in connection with the dredging and widening of the River Yarra. The fourth locomotive to arrive was builders No. 7860 (of 1886) which was also originally destined for the M.H.T., but was purchased by C & E. Millar instead. Millars had won the contract for the construction of the Palmerston (Port Darwin) to Pine Creek railway in the Northern Territory and in 1887 this locomotive was transferred to Darwin.

Shortly after its arrival in Darwin it acquired the nickname *Sandfly*, a name it has retained to this day. *Sandfly* was used for shunting duties around the wharf at Palmerston until the contract was completed in October 1889. The South Australian Railways then acquired the locomotive and it was officially allocated the road No. 107 .

The railway was transferred to the Commonwealth on 1st January 1911, but was still worked by the S.A.R. However, on 1st July 1918 No. 107 was officially transferred to Commonwealth Railways stock and was renumbered NA1.

No. 107 was later transferred to the Commonwealth Railways and renumbered NA1. However, it is probably better known by its nickname "Sandfly".

(Unknown/Ron Stewien collection)

It was continually used for shunting at the wharf, yard and workshops in Darwin until about 1942-43 when it was set aside at Parap workshops. Because of the war and the vulnerability of the railway workshops in Darwin they were moved to Katherine and NA1 was later transferred as well. It evidently spent the rest of its working life at Katherine before being written off in June 1950.

For some reason it was then transferred to Port Augusta where it was eventually renovated and then placed on display on the platform at Port Augusta station. It remained there from 1960 until 1982. With the transfer of some of Australian National's facilities to Adelaide NA1 was again moved, fully restored, and in May 1984 was placed on display at A.N's new Adelaide Rail Passenger Terminal at Keswick.

Incidentally other locomotives of this type saw service in Western Australia. One of them, Baldwin builders No. 7111, was originally used by the Melbourne Harbour Trust, but was sold to Millars Timber & Trading Company and put to work at their Denmark Mill in April 1897. It was named *Kia-Ora* following an extensive overhaul at Yarloop workshops in 1905. *Kia-Ora* then spent most of its working life at Carnarvon and in the Bunbury area before being taken out of traffic in 1960. It was donated to the Australian Railway Historical Society (W.A. Division) in July 1962 and can now be seen at their Bassendean Railway Museum.

Introduced	:	1889 (SAR)	Heating Surface	:	
Builder:	:	Baldwin	Tubes		
Driving Wheel	:	2ft 4in.	Superheater	:	-
Bogie Wheel	:	-	Firebox	:	
Weight in W.O.	:	9 tons	Grate Area	:	
Max. Axle Load	:	4tons 10cwt.	Boiler Pressure	:	140lb./sq in.

Length	:	18ft 6in.	Tractive Effort	:	3,270lb.
Water	:	330 gallons	Cylinders	:	2(O) 8 x 12in.
Total	:	1 (SAR)	Coal	:	4cwt.

No.	Bldr.No.	In Service	Condemned	Notes
107	Bdwn/7860	12/1889	1/1/1911	To C.R.as NA1, cond. 6/1950

Z193 was one of ten beautifully proportioned Z class 4-4-0s.   *(Ron Stewien collection).*

Z Class   4-4-0

The beautifully proportioned Z class are now part of history. They were the only purpose built passenger locomotives used on the narrow gauge as well as being the only 4-4-0s. They were a small class of ten locomotives and it is very unfortunate that none survive.

The Z class was designed at Islington and the initial group of eight were built by James Martin & Co., of Gawler. When placed in service they were all allocated to the Northern Division primarily for working the *Broken Hill Express* between Cockburn and Terowie. Two additional locomotives, Nos. 195 and 196, were constructed at Islington and entered traffic during 1911.

In addition to the *Broken Hill Express,* which later became the domain of the larger T class, the Z class are believed to have worked on the former Western Division between Moonta, Hamley Bridge and Gladstone until just prior to gauge conversion in the 1920s. Gauge conversion of this division meant a surplus of narrow gauge motive power in the north and three of the class were transferred to the South East during 1924. No. 193 was transferred on 9th March 1924, No. 195 on 18th December and No. 196 on 27th December. They were followed by 189 and 191 during 1926.

Z class No. 192. *(Unknown/Ron Stewien collection)*

The unusual internal combustion locomotive No. 259. *(Author's collection)*

With their heavy axle load of 9tons 17cwt they were not permitted to work over the lightly laid lines in the South East and were therefore restricted to the Wolseley to Mount Gambier main line. The last of the class to leave Peterborough for the South East was No. 192, which wasn't transferred until 13th August 1940.

With six of the class in the South East this left only Nos. 187, 188, 190 and 194 at Peterborough where they remained until the early 1940s. All four were recorded as being at Islington in January 1942, although they were still officially allocated to Peterborough as late as June 1948. Of the six in the South East only three were available for traffic; the other three were still classified as serviceable, but they had been placed in storage.

The South East locomotives survived until gauge conversion during the 1950s. No. 195 was transferred to Port Lincoln in February 1950, No. 191 in March 1950 and 192 in July 1950. These three locomotives had the distinction of being allocated to all three narrow gauge divisions. However, their time at Port Lincoln was short lived and they were condemned in the mid 1950s. In fact, all of the Z class were condemned in 1956.

This small class received only a few modifications during their lives. Such things as electric lighting were fitted during the late 1920s, their smokeboxes were extended, the slim tapered chimney was replaced with a parallel one and with their relegation to lesser duties their bar frame cow catchers were progressively removed from 1953. In addition extra boards were fitted to their tenders to increase coal capacity.

Like the broad gauge S class we have to be content with photographs of these fine machines.

Introduced	:	1894	Heating Surface	:	
Builders	:	JM & Isl.	Tubes	:	795.22sq ft.
Driving Wheel	:	4ft 6in.	Superheater	:	-
Bogie Wheel	:	2ft 3in.	Firebox	:	73.93sq ft.
Weight in W.O.	:	50tons 1cwt.	Grate Area	:	13.87sq ft.
Max. Axle Load	:	9tons 17cwt.	Boiler Pressure	:	145lb./sq in.
Length	:	41ft 10⅛in.	Tractive Effort	:	10,270lb.
Water	:	1,600 gallons	Cylinders	:	2(O) 15 x 20in.
Total	:	10	Coal	:	4tons 10cwt.

No.	Bldr/No.	In Service	Condemned	Notes
187	JM/99	22/12/1894	23/1/1956	Northern Division loco
188	JM/100	9/1/1895	23/1/1956	Northern Division loco
189	JM/101	5/2/1895	23/1/1956	Northern & South East
190	JM/102	20/2/1895	23/1/1956	Northern Division loco
191	JM/103	26/2/1895	16/10/1956	Condemned at Port Lincoln
192	JM/104	26/2/1895	16/10/1956	Condemned at Port Lincoln
193	JM/105	26/3/1895	23/1/1956	Northern & South East
194	JM/106	3/4/1895	23/1/1956	Northern Division loco
195	Isl/18	29/9/1911	16/10/1956	Condemned at Port Lincoln
196	Isl/19	23/10/1911	23/1/1956	Northern & South East

No. 259   0-6-0

The first internal combustion locomotive owned by the South Australian Railways and used on the narrow gauge was this rather primitive machine which was built by Ironside, Son & Dykerhoff of London. Little is known about it except that it was used at Port Lincoln and apparently was not very successful.

Evidently someone decided to take No. 259 for a run on the main line where it bent one of its axles. The locomotive was never repaired and it is believed the prime mover was sent back to Islington workshops where it was used to power a lathe for many years.

From the photograph No. 259 looks a rather ungainly machine. It lasted on the S.A.R. less than ten years and made no significant contribution to the evolution of the internal combustion railway locomotive in South Australia.

Introduced	:	1914 (SAR)	Power	:	100 BHP (300 r.p.m.)
Builder	:	Ironside	Tractive Effort	:	7,500lb.
Driving Wheel	:	2ft 3 3/16in.	Weight	:	20tons
Total	:	1			

No.	Bldr./No,	In Service	Condemned	Notes
259	Irn/163	6/6/1914	13/7/1923	Used at Port Lincoln

No. 260   0-4-0ST

Apart from the locomotives used around the mines at Wallaroo there were very few small narrow gauge four coupled tank locomotives in service in South Australia. However, No. 260 was a typical example of this type. It was built by Hudswell Clark & Co. in 1911 and purchased new by the Engineer-in-Chief's department and initially used on the Woakwine Range Main Drainage Channel, near Beachport. This was part of the South East Drainage Scheme where it was employed hauling side tipping wagons to and from the workings.

On completion of the work in the South East this locomotive was transferred to the South Australian Railways and placed in service on the Northern Division. It assumed the road number 260 then.

Shortly afterwards it could be found at Wallaroo where it shared shunting duties with the V class 0-4-4WTs already stationed there. It was used in the yard and out on the jetty shunting grain wagons. The loco crews at Wallaroo preferred No. 260 to the V class and it was remembered by them with great affection. They claimed it was a more powerful locomotive and much better to work on.

With the gauge conversion of the Western Division in the mid 1920s it was evidently returned to Peterborough and again used for shunting before being sold in June 1936. Its subsequent history and ultimate fate are not known.

Introduced	:	1916 (S.A.R.)	Heating Surface	:	
Builder	:	Hudswell Clark	Tubes	:	254.4sq ft.
Driving Wheel	:	2ft 9½in.	Superheater	:	-
Bogie Wheel	:	-	Firebox	:	33.2sq ft.
Weight in W.O.	:	15tons 18cwt.	Grate Area	:	5.6sq ft.
Max. Axle Load	:	7tons 19cwt.	Boiler Pressure	:	160lb./sq in.
Length	:	20ft 2¼in.	Tractive Effort	:	6,494lb.
Water	:	390 gallons	Cylinders	:	2(O) 10 x 16in.
Total	:	1	Coal	:	10cwt.

No.	Bldr./No.	In Service	Condemned	Notes
260	HC/965	30/9/1916	6/1936	Built 1911

Hudswell Clark 0-4-0ST No. 260.   *(Author's collection)*

300 Class   4-8-2+2-8-4

Although W.A. Webb had considered a replacement for the T class during the 1920s there were to be no new locomotive acquisitions on the narrow gauge until the early 1950s. With the gauge conversion of the Western Division there was in fact a surplus of motive power which meant that good serviceable locomotives were transferred to replace older types, while others were disposed of.

It was not until the late 1940s that the demand from the traffic branch strained the locomotive departments resources. A replacement locomotive type was required for the ore traffic from Cockburn which would in turn allow the T class to concentrate on Leigh Creek coal traffic. Ten 400 class Beyer Garratts were ordered from England during 1951, but because of delays and the urgent need for additional motive power six secondhand Australian Standard Garratts were purchased from the Western Australian Government Railways as a temporary measure.

The A.S.G. story began back in the late 1930s, when the increase in traffic, because of the outbreak of World War II severely taxed the resources of the narrow gauge railways throughout Australia. In all fifty seven A.S.Gs were completed and the first entered service on Queensland Government Railways in 1943. The Government railway workshops at Islington (S.A.R.), Newport (V.R.) and Midland (W.A.G.R.) and the Clyde Engineering Company's Sydney works built the entire class of sixty five, but eight (Nos. G34 to G36 and G39 to G43) were never assembled.

Page 170: 304 and 303, two of the unpopular A.S.Gs at Peterborough, 28th January 1953.
(Ron Stewien)

The A.S.Gs were numbered G1 to G65 and they were issued to traffic on Tasmanian Government Railways and Western Australian Government Railways as well as the Q.G.R. However, they were rather hurriedly built to an untried design and unfortunately in their early days were fraught with mechanical problems. In fact the Q.G.R. had taken all of their A.S.Gs out of traffic within a couple of years.

In West Australia there was so much ill feeling between the Union and W.A.G.R. that a Royal Commission was held between November 1945 and April 1946 to establish the safety, economy and effectiveness of the A.S.G. and then to advise whether the locomotives should be taken out of traffic, or modifications made. The result was that many of the Union's claims were considered justified and the W.A.G.R. made the suggested modifications to the class between January 1947 and August 1948, as well as further improvements of their own.

From February 1948 some of the W.A.G.R. locomotives were converted to oil burning because of the coal strikes and price increases in the late 1940s. However, the introduction of the Pm, Pmr and W classes resulted in the first of W.A.G.R.s twenty five A.S.Gs being withdrawn in 1951. Others followed and with the arrival of the V class steam and X and XA class diesels they were further displaced. The last surviving A.S.G. in Western Australia was withdrawn in January 1957.

The Tasmanian Government Railways persevered with the A.S.G. and overcame most of their problems. They continued using A.S.Gs until the late 1950s. The Emu Bay Railway purchased three secondhand A.S.Gs and they ran until 1964.

Australian Portland Cement Company purchased A.S.G. No. G33 (APC No.3) in 1946 for use on their Fyansford railway. In 1968 this locomotive was handed over for preservation at the North Williamstown museum and is the only one of the class to have survived.

In 1952 the S.A.R. purchased six redundant A.S.Gs from the W.A.G.R. Their condition at the time was considered poor and after some work was undertaken at Islington they were transferred to Terowie and then Peterborough for final assembly. The distinctive cowling on the top of the boiler, (to the rear of the chimney) had been removed by W.A.G.R. It was necessary to fit air brakes before they could be used on the S.A.R. At some stage further conversions to oil burning were made.

At Islington their A.S.G. numbers were removed and they were renumbered in the 300 series.

A.S.G. No.	In Service W.A.G.R.	Conv. to oil	W/drawn	S.A.R. No.
G26	22/11/1943	-	7/11/1951	305
G29	10/3/1944	-	24/2/1951	302
G30	5/4/1944	-	7/11/1951	304
G31	2/3/1945	13/2/1948	6/2/1951	303
G32	1/6/1945	5/3/1948	31/10/1951	300
G49	20/10/1944	-	14/11/1951	301

The 300 class were based at Peterborough and put to work on ore traffic from Cockburn to Belalie North, but they soon earned themselves a reputation for unreliability. Problems with rods bending, losing springs, hot cabs and overheating axleboxes all added to their already tarnished reputations. Loco crews complained to the authorities, but they were assured the 300 class were only a stopgap measure until the new locomotives ordered from Beyer Peacock arrived.

A few minor modifications were made at Peterborough and sieves were fitted in their front tanks. The locomotive number was added above the front headlight after they had been placed in service. An instruction was issued by the S.A.R. that the 300 class were only to be used chimney first when under load, except between Terowie and Peterborough.

Shortly after the arrival of the 400 class Garratts the 300s were taken out of traffic. All were condemned by the end of 1954, although they were not officially withdrawn until two years later, when they were sold to H.G. Smith of Alberton for scrap. Such was the haste to get rid of these unpopular locomotives. However, their water tanks were retained at Peterborough, mounted on flat wagons and used during times of drought.

The A.S.G. was a failed attempt to produce a standard locomotive. However, a little more time spent on planning and trialling before mass production would have given these locomotives a better chance, but history cannot be changed.

Introduced	:	1952 (SAR)	Heating Surface	:	
Builder	:	WAGR & VR	Tubes	:	1,535sq ft.
Driving Wheel	:	4ft 0in.	Superheater	:	355sq ft.
Bogie Wheel	:	2ft 6in.	Firebox	:	163sq ft.
Weight in W.O.	:	119tons	Grate Area	:	35sq ft.
Max. Axle Load	:	9tons 2cwt.	Boiler Pressure	:	200lb./sq in.
Length	:	85ft 6¾ in.	Tractive Effort	:	34,510lb.
Water	:	4,200 gallons	Cylinders	:	4(O) 14¼ x 24in.
Total	:	6	Oil	:	1,600 gallons

No.	Bldr./No.	In Service	Withdrawn	Notes
300	VR	19/3/1952	24/2/1956	A.S.G. No. G32
301	WAGR	23/4/1952	24/2/1956	A.S.G. No. G49
302	WAGR	2/7/1952	24/2/1956	A.S.G. No. G29
303	VR	12/9/1952	24/2/1956	A.S.G. No. G31
304	WAGR	13/9/1952	24/2/1956	A.S.G. No. G30
305	WAGR	5/11/1952	24/2/1956	A.S.G. No. G26

303 at Peterborough, January 1953.   *(Ron Stewien)*

Newly arrived No. 409 was still minus chimney, dome cover and other fittings when photographed at Port Pirie during 1954. *(Ron Stewien)*

400 Class   4-8-2+2-8-4

Beyer Peacock & Co., had pioneered the articulated Beyer Garratt design and in 1909 produced the first locomotive of this type for the Tasmanian Government Railways. The Garratt principle involves two sets of wheels, motion and cylinders with one boiler suspended between them. This allowed for maximum power and adhesion with a low axle loading, a combination ideally suited for lightly laid lines with high density traffic.

Garratts were used all around the world with countries as far apart as Brazil, Russia and South Africa using them with great success, but up until the early 1950s there were no examples on the South Australian Railways.

During 1951 ten locomotives were ordered from Beyer Peacock & Co. Their design was based on some metre gauge Garratts built by Beyer Peacock for the British War Department during World War II. They had similar dimensions to the East African Railways 60th class and the Indian Railways GX class. The 60th class in particular were almost identical and apart from a few exterior fittings could easily have been mistaken for one of the new 400 class.

The 400 class were not large by Garratt standards, especially when compared with the mighty East African Railways 59th class with its 21 ton axle load and 83,350lb tractive effort, but they were one of the most successful lightweight Garratt designs ever built. However, they were still the most powerful narrow gauge steam locomotives used on a government railway in Australia. Although supplied to the narrow gauge they could be easily converted to either standard or 5ft 3in gauges.

173

Beyer Peacock licensed construction of the 400s to Societe Franco-Belge De Material Des Chemins De Fer, of Raismes, France. The first batch arrived aboard the ship *Belnor* in 1953 and they were placed in service during June and July that year. The final five were issued to traffic during January and February 1954.

After the failure of the locally built 300 class Garratts the arrival of the new 400 class was met with some apprehension. However, they soon lived down the reputation of the 300 class and were used successfully on ore and heavy goods trains between Cockburn and Port Pirie. They also saw service on the *Broken Hill Express* and goods trains between Peterborough and Terowie. In their latter years they occasionally worked the local passenger train between Peterborough and Terowie. This was a rather overpowered working as it often consisted of one carriage and a brakevan, with the odd goods wagon or two. The whole train weighing less than the locomotive hauling it!

The 400s ventured onto the Quorn line in the late 1960s on ballast trains to Black Rock. One of the class, No. 402, worked the regular goods right through to Quorn on 31st October 1968, but this was never apparently repeated.

Following the introduction of the 830 class diesel electric locomotives to the Peterborough Division during 1963 most of the Garratts were taken out of traffic and placed into storage. Only 406 and 409 were still in use by September 1967; the rest were kept in serviceable condition as they would be required again to take over from the narrow gauge diesels while they were being converted to standard gauge.

In February 1968 the 400s were still being occasionally used, mainly working ballast trains to Terowie, Black Rock and Yunta, but were only utilised when 830 class diesel electrics were unavailable. Later that year, with the construction of the new standard gauge line nearing completion, some of the stored locomotives were put back into service. In all six of the class, Nos. 400, 401, 402, 404, 406 and 409 were in use during 1969 and they were again regularly allotted to ore train working. This short reprieve lasted until 10th January 1970 when narrow gauge workings on the Cockburn to Port Pirie line ceased. Garratt 404 headed the last narrow gauge steam train out of Port Pirie. The 400 class era had come to an end.

All ten of the class were built as oil burners, which certainly made life much easier for the fireman. However, their oil tanks were removable and provision was made for the fitting of a mechanical stocker should they ever be converted to coal burning.

Although narrow gauge steam locomotives were painted black the division was so proud of the 400 class that they were given a coat of what was to become known as Peterborough's invisible green paint. By mixing a little green into the black paint it produced a rather unusual toning which in certain lighting did appear to be a very dark green shade. Also when the locomotives had been stored in the open for a while and the paint became weathered the green pigment became quite clear.

Only minor modifications were made to these locomotives in traffic and most of these were in the early years. During their first year in traffic it was necessary to modify the oil feed delivery pipes to the side rods and the generator's steam exhaust outlet.

From 1954 new blow off cock mufflers were fitted and the cylinder relief valves were redesigned. There was a concern over oil fumes escaping from the firehole door and the hind unit driving wheels had a tendency to skid. The necessary precautionary instructions were issued.

406 refuelling at Peterborough loco.

(John Southwell)

Class leader No. 400 pictured shortly after entering service.   (Ron Stewien)

In 1955 the blower valve was replaced with a standard S.A.R. type. Also modifications were made to the radius rod, the firebricks were rearranged in the firebox, the centre fastener for the coupled springs was altered and exhaust nozzles were modified. The number of bolts were also increased in the bottom flange of the chimney.

Brackets to carry connecting rods in the event of a breakdown were fitted to the locomotives from 1956 and in 1958 the locking device on the firehole door was modified to prevent rattling.

When working from Peterborough to Cockburn an instruction was issued that the 400 class should work chimney first and deliver their load to Burns yard. The engine would then be turned for the return journey. In the early 1960s they were also permitted to use the Paratoo triangle to turn.

The 400 class were allowed to haul 1,100 tons between Cockburn and Paratoo. At Paratoo a T class was attached for the remainder of the journey to Peterborough, otherwise the load had to be reduced to 900 tons as the ruling grade between Paratoo and Peterborough was 1 in 80.

The load between Peterborough and Belalie North for a 400 and T class was again 1,100 tons. After Belalie North either the 400 or T was allowed to take the load unassisted to Port Pirie.

While the 400 class regularly worked on the Cockburn line only one of the class ever worked over Silverton Tramway metals to Broken Hill. While hauling the *Farewell Narrow Gauge* special train No. 402, assisted by T class No. 243, entered Broken Hill on 12th October 1969.

During their short time on the South Australian Railways the 400 class Garratts had rather uneventful lives. The notable exception being the rollover of 408 near Paratoo while hauling train No. 222 the Peterborough bound *Broken Hill Express*. This incident occurred on the 27th December 1960 and unfortunately claimed a fatality. The locomotive, five vans and two carriages were derailed and the leading bogie of sleeping car *Nilpena* also left the track.

Although 400 class workings ceased in January 1970 the boiler from No. 405 was to see further use in the S.A.R. laundry in Adelaide. It was removed from its frame and then sent to Adelaide in September 1966. The boiler frame was left at Terowie while the front and rear sections were placed in the condemned locomotive sidings at Peterborough. The laundry was demolished in March 1981 and the boiler disposed of.

The 400 class era ended well before its time. They still had years of useful life left in them. To the casual observer they were fascinating machines which epitomised the power of steam. Although their enclosed cabs became rather warm in summer the Garratts were still popular with crews. Their sheer brute strength was unmatched on the narrow gauge.

The survivors lasted for a couple of years after the end of steam in the scrap ranks at Peterborough, but fortunately two of the class have been preserved. No. 402 was reserved for the Lithgow Zig Zag Railway (New South Wales) and was stored in Peterborough roundhouse until it was transferred to Lithgow in December 1976. No. 409 was transferred to the Mile End Railway Museum shortly after withdrawal. It entered the museum in November 1970. In 1988, together with all the other museum exhibits, it was transferred to the new Port Dock Station Railway Museum at Port Adelaide.

Introduced	:	1953	Heating Surface	:	
Builder	:	S.F-B	Tubes	:	1,779sq ft.
Driving Wheel	:	4ft.	Superheater	:	370sq ft.
Bogie Wheel	:	2ft 4 1/2in.	Firebox	:	193sq ft.
Weight in W.O.	:	148tons 19cwt 3qr.	Grate Area	:	48.75sq ft.
Max. Axle Load	:	10tons 13cwt 2qr.	Boiler Pressure	:	200 1b./sq in.
Length	:	87ft 5in.	Tractive Effort	:	43,520 1b.
Water	:	3,700 gallons	Cylinders	:	4(O) 16 x 24in.
Total	:	10	Oil	:	1,400gals.

No.	Bldr./No.	In Service	Withdrawn	Notes
400	S.F-B/2973	8/7/1953	1/5/1970	BP B/No. 7622
401	S.F-B/2974	1/7/1953	1/5/1970	BP B/No. 7623
402	S.F-B/2975	16/7/1953	1/5/1970	BP B/No. 7624. Preserved
403	S.F-B/2976	29/6/1953	12/8/1969	BP B/No. 7625
404	S.F-B/2977	23/7/1953	1/5/1970	BP B/No. 7626
405	S.F-B/2978	21/1/1954	7/6/1966	BP B/No. 7627
406	S.F-B/2979	13/2/1954	1/5/1970	BP B/No. 7628
407	S.F-B/2980	30/1/1954	12/8/1969	BP B/No. 7629
408	S.F-B/2981	15/1/1954	12/8/1969	BP B/No. 7630
409	S.F-B/2982	6/2/1954	1/5/1970	BP B/No. 7631. Preserved

830 Class   Co-Co

One of the most versatile and widely used diesel locomotive types in Australia is the Goodwin-Alco model DL 531. They were purchased in large numbers by the New South

Wales and South Australian government railways. The Silverton Tramway Company also purchased three of this type to replace its entire steam locomotive fleet. In New South Wales they were known as the 48 class and in South Australia the 830 class.

The 830 class were purchased for working secondary railway lines on goods and mixed traffic duties, but were equally at home on passenger and main line work. The class have been used on all three railway gauges in South Australia and from the early 1980s some of them were transferred to Tasmania by their current owners, Australian National.

They were all built by A.E. Goodwin of Sydney under license to Alco (U.S.A.). The first of the class officially entered service on the S.A.R. in December 1959. Another nine followed during 1960, but all of these early units were issued to the Murray Bridge Division broad gauge lines.

The 830 class was also chosen to replace steam on the narrow gauge Peterborough and Port Lincoln divisions. The first two, Nos. 850 and 851, were issued to Port Lincoln in March and April 1962 respectively. They were a considerable improvement over the ageing T class on this division and further acquisitions followed. By 1970 a total of nine of the class, Nos. 850 to 855, 871 to 873, were at Port Lincoln, with another two (856 and 857) transferred later that year from Peterborough.

On the narrow gauge the 830 class became known locally as the 850 class, but this was frowned upon by the hierarchy at Islington so officially they reverted to the 830 designation.

To replace the 400 class Garratts and T class on mainline duties on the Peterborough Division the first 830s arrived in February 1963. They took over the heavy ore traffic from Cockburn to Port Pirie as well as mainline goods and the *Broken Hill Express*.

830 class No. 851 at Port Lincoln, 27th August 1977. (Steve McNicol)

866 at Laura, 9th February 1980. By this time the piping shrike had been removed from the 830s based at Gladstone by Australian National.   *(Steve McNicol)*

On ore trains they were commonly used in tandem hauling up to 2,400 tons out of Cockburn. Later they were used on the Wilmington and Quorn lines. 857 worked the first diesel hauled train to Wilmington on 5th August 1968, but just over four years prior to that it hauled the last Radium Hill to Cutana goods before this line was abandoned. This actually occurred on 28th July 1964.

The Peterborough Division locomotives were taken out of traffic late in 1969 for conversion to standard gauge. Other gauge swapping occurred during S.A.R. ownership and today the 830 class are still being moved around to suit traffic requirements.

With the closure of the narrow gauge Cockburn to Port Pirie line four of the class were retained to work the Peterborough to Quorn and Gladstone to Wilmington lines. Nos. 858 and 867 were based at Peterborough with 865 and 866 at Gladstone. With the lack of traffic on the Quorn line 858 was transferred to the broad gauge on 12th June 1973 leaving only 867 at Peterborough.

After the transfer of the S.A.R. country railway lines to Australian National Railways, and the closure of the narrow gauge line to Alice Springs a few years later, redundant locomotives of the NSU and NT classes were transferred to Peterborough and Gladstone to release the 830s for more productive work elsewhere on the system.

About the same time the NJ class were transferred to Port Lincoln to release the 830s for further work in Tasmania, but more recently some 830s have gone back to Port Lincoln.

The 830 class have had varied and interesting careers and most are still active. However, their history under A.N. ownership is another story. Although the class totalled forty five locomotives, including Silverton Tramway No. 27 purchased secondhand in 1970, only those that were used on the narrow gauge by the S.A.R. have been listed in the following tables. Transfers during Australian National ownership are not recorded either.

Introduced	:	1962 (ng)	Model	:	DL 531G
Builder	:	A.E. Goodwin	Engine	:	Alco 251
Driving Wheel	:	3ft 4in.	Cylinders	:	(6) 9 x 10½in.
Length	:	48ft 5in.	Power	:	(840,850-855)
Max. Axle Load	:	11tons 11cwt.			900hp.
Total Weight	:	69tons 6cwt.			(856-873) 975hp.
Water (cooling)	:	92 gallons	Tractive Effort	:	40,200lb cont.
Gearing	:	92:19	Sand Capacity	:	10cu ft.
Lubricating Oil	:	117 gallons	Max. Speed	:	75mph.
Total (on ng)	:	22 (SAR)	Fuel Capacity	:	500 gallons

No.	In Service	Left N.G.	Notes
840	28/3/1967	3/2/1970	Issued to Broad Gauge 22/5/1962 - NG P'boro
850	30/3/1962	-	Issued to Port Lincoln
851	19/4/1962	-	Issued to Port Lincoln
852	30/9/1963	-	Issued to Port Lincoln
853	10/10/1963	-	Issued to Port Lincoln
854	23/9/1963	-	Issued to Port Lincoln
855	11/10/1963	-	Issued to Port Lincoln
856	12/2/1963	-	Issued to Peterborough - to P/L 8/5/1970
857	29/4/1963	-	Issued to Peterborough - to P/L 4/5/1970
858	9/5/1963	12/6/1973	Issued to Peterborough - Quorn line
859	25/5/1963	12/1/1970	Issued to Peterborough
860	27/5/1963	12/1/1970	Issued to Peterborough
861	7/6/1963	12/1/1970	Issued to Peterborough
862	20/6/1963	12/1/1970	Issued to Peterborough
863	28/6/1963	12/1/1970	Issued to Peterborough
864	11/7/1963	12/1/1970	Issued to Peterborough
865	18/7/1963	-	Issued to Peterborough - Wilmington line
866	25/7/1963	-	Issued to Peterborough - Wilmington line
867	8/8/1963	-	Issued to Peterborough - Quorn line
871	3/2/1966	-	Issued to Port Lincoln
872	7/3/1966	-	Issued to Port Lincoln
873	22/4/1966	-	Issued to Port Lincoln

* * * * * * * * * * *

Rear cover (top): 400 class No. 408 was photographed while in storage at Peterborough, 7th October 1967. This locomotive was never returned to traffic and was cut up for scrap. Its rather weathered paintwork gives some indication of the 'invisible green' livery applied to the 400 class.

(Steve McNicol)

Rear cover (bottom): At Port Lincoln the T class era had just about come to an end when T209 and T48 were photographed awaiting the cutters torch, 30th June 1970.

(Steve McNicol)

ACKNOWLEDGMENTS

Due to the lack of space in this book acknowledgments, reference sources and other information will be printed in Narrow Gauge Memories - the Experience. However, we would like to thank all of those who have contributed to this publication.